PROJECT MANAGEMENT

A Quick Start Beginner's Guide For The Serious Project Manager To Managing Any Project Easily

Donald J. Scott

Table of Contents

Introduction

Chances are you have heard of Project Management. In fact, many people have heard of it, but in very loose context. Some people think of project management in terms of managing people – checking that they report early for work and they stay at work till the official closing time; they work efficiently; and so on. However, there is more to project management than managing people. You have resources to plan and budget for; stakeholders to consult; contingency measures to consider; and a lot more.

In this book, *Project Management: How to Be a Successful Project Manager,* you get to learn everything that you need to know as a project manager. For instance, you get to learn what the role of a project manager is; how to plan for a project; how to execute it effectively; and so on. Today, businesses that are taking the lead in their respective industries are those that have appreciated the value of a competent project manager. At the end of the day, the overall success of an organization is the sum total of different successful projects.

Happy reading and all the best as you sharpen your project management skills!

Chapter 1: What Is Project Management?

Can anyone really speak of how to manage something before they know what that thing really is? It just won't be possible. In our case, you have got to understand what a project is before you can speak of project management.

So, What, Exactly, Is A Project?

Well, look at it as some endeavor of a temporary nature, with a planned start time as well as a planned end time, and whose end result is pre-defined, say, creation of a unique product or service. In short, a project is a specific endeavor with a scope that is clearly defined and resources that are set aside specifically for its implementation; also whose end result you can foretell. See why it is being said to be temporary?

Also, look at a project as an undertaking that is unique because in actual fact there is nothing routine about it. The operations involved are specific and are meant to help you fulfill a given goal. In fact, in a project, you usually form a working team of people that you normally do not work with; people who, on other days, do diverse things. They may even be people, who ordinarily live in different geographical zones; even probably working for diverse organizations.

Examples of Projects

With the explanation given above, you will be able to see how the undertakings below fit the bill; hence qualifying to be termed as projects:

- Development of some specific software meant to improve business

- Construction of a specific bridge

- Construction of a specific building

- Organized relief effort following some natural disaster

- Introduction of a product into a new geographical market

Some factors that are pertinent to a project include:

- Timely delivery of results

- Keeping within the budget

- Achieving the learning intended

- Achieving the intended integration

To succeed in achieving the above objectives, management of the project must be top notch.

So What Is Project Management?

You can simply explain project management as doing whatever is necessary – use of knowledge; employment of skills and tools; as well as application of appropriate techniques – to accomplish the activities that comprise the project as per requirements. As you can see, project management is something you may have done one time or another – or even many times – without necessarily giving it a definition. People are often doing it informally.

However, it is advisable to address specific projects in a kind of formal way, especially where there are significant resources involved. In any case, in today's world, resources are always scarce and you want to ensure that you are using whatever is at your disposal optimally. That way, you can manage to accomplish a lot and succeed with limited resources. The subject of project management actually became formal in the middle of the 20th century and has been taken seriously ever since.

It will be relatively easy to understand project management if we break it down to semi-independent stages.

Here Are the Stages of Project Management

The main stages in project management are broadly five. They include:

1. The initiating stage

2. The planning stage

3. The stage of execution

4. The stage of monitoring as well as controlling

5. The closing stage

Now, there are so many things that you could do with your resources, even as an organization, and unless you have a structured way of assessing your choices, you may end up embarking on projects that are least helpful to you in terms of success. Project management experts advise that you base your considerations on six major reasons.

Here they are:

Demand in the market

Under market demand, you initiate a project to fulfill an existing need. For instance, you don't embark on producing a set of products and then begin looking for buyers. A good example is when a country realizes that its power supply is not enough for its citizens; or that it is too expensive for most of them. There is good reason here to initiate an alternative power project. If the country relies mainly on hydro-electric power, it may organize to begin a wind based power project.

And if clean water sources are getting depleted or their supply is not enough for a growing population, then state bodies or private firms may find it worthwhile to invest in water recycling projects. In both of these cases, a need has been identified. The market is ready for the output – in our case cheaper power and clean water.

But generally speaking, how do you know what the market

really wants or if there's demand for your planned product or service? We'll talk about that in a bit.

Business related need

The kind of need being referred to when we speak of it being business related is one where existing businesses will find it necessary to consume your service or your product. If using the service makes a business more credible to customers; improves a business' efficiency in a way that facilitates it to beat the competition hands down; or serves businesses in a markedly better way; it is worth initiating a project for.

For good examples in this category, think of ISO certification, which is the certification given to an organization by the International Organization for Standardization for maintaining high quality standards. You can embark on a project to acquire ISO certification, knowing quite well that business of substance is, very likely, going to make you the go-to organization. We are talking of business credibility and visibility here.

You can also think of a Database Management System (DMS) as a project, which when undertaken, would improve your business efficiency by virtue of the business being able to retrieve accurate data as need arises. Remember when you get important information in a timely manner you are able to seize business opportunities before many of your competitors. In fact, you would be right to think of this aspect of business need the way you would a strategic opportunity. It means you are initiating the project to prepare yourself for future advantage.

Specific Customer Order

If your business deals in carpentry, why would you not begin to make, for instance, a specific number of chairs if a certain customer asked for them? Even if your normal daily activities involve making a variety of wooden stuff, this particular time you are specifically going to concentrate of the number of chairs that this customer wants, and make them in the design that the customer prefers. That is a project on its own.

Technology based project

What investor wants his or her businesses continuing to transact in the old school manual way when every other business is computerized and doing their daily transactions electronically? Obviously, one who is not ambitious and forward looking... But any person seeking to be efficient today, whether in business, in research, and everything else you can think of, needs to be able to choose appropriate technology. In that light, individuals and organizations are always initiating technology related projects.

Legal obligation

Legal obligation or requirement calls for particular projects to be initiated in order to have the legal obligation met. When, for instance, government passes a law that demands all public transport vehicles to be fitted with speed governors, shrewd entrepreneurs see a business opportunity where they can initiate projects to manufacture governors. Had the government not made it a legal obligation to have the gadgets fitted in public service vehicles, there would be no need for such projects. So, essentially, the projects under this category are initiated courtesy of the law.

The same case has applied in the recent past when most countries have been making a switch of their television operations from analogue to digital. As such, entrepreneurs in many countries have initiated projects to manufacture digital boxes for sale to individuals so that they can use them in their homes and business premises for TV digitization.

Social Need

This is the kind of need that motivates people to initiate a project that benefits all of them; or the community in general. If, for instance, parents have agreed on specific spots where their children can congregate as they await the school bus or whatever other vehicle takes the kids to and from school, it is only reasonable that they should think of initiating a project to build shelters in those respective locations. The social need here is automatic because in the few minutes that the children wait for the transport, it could rain. They may also be too tired to keep standing, in which case some of them may wish to sit down; thus the need for a suitable shelter.

Chapter 2: Estimating And Forecasting Market Demand

Regardless of the industry that you're in, it is important that you know how to estimate the market demand for your company's products or services as a product manager. So how do you actually go about estimating market demand? Here are a few tips on how you can do so.

Market - based point of view

From this particular perspective, you'll need to ask yourself: how many are the prospects for your products or services? And when we say prospects, we aren't just talking about potential customers. We are talking of people who are interested in your product or service. Unlike the usual product-based approach, which takes into consideration only the product or services volume, this approach estimates how much is the demand for your product or service.

Using the market-based approach, you begin by estimating the most number of prospects. Let's say that you're into providing financial consultancy services for business owners. To estimate the market demand for your product, you begin with the highest-level definition of your market, which is all businesses that make use of financial consultant services either as mandated by law or by the nature of their business. Let's say that at most, these firms total 10,000 prospects.

The next lower level is estimated by filtering out some of those prospects that are already locked in 12-month contracts with other financial consultancy services and that these number around 5,000 prospects. This means that your prospects have gone down to just 5,000.

At the next lower level, you can further filter out your prospects. Let's say that out of the remaining 5,000, only 2,500 are in the market for financial consultancy services. This further brings down your market to just 2,500 potential customers. This then is your estimated market demand for your financial consultancy service.

In the above-mentioned illustration, a top-down approach to identifying market demand was utilized. And to better understand the demand for your products or services, you can also need to know and manage several market-related forces that can affect the demand or market potential for your products or services. These market-related forces include:

- Awareness of your products or services including their benefits.

- Your products or services' availability in certain locations.

- Your prospects' ability to utilize your products or services, i.e., the resources and knowledge that is available to them so that they can properly use your products/services.

- Benefit insufficiency, which pertains to some of your products or services' benefits that may not be relevant for a particular subset of your prospects.

- Your products or services' prices, i.e., affordability.

Market growth is another factor that's very relevant when it comes to forecasting and planning your products and services' demand, which you'll also need to consider as a project manager. In particular, we're talking about the growth of the whole market, which you can estimate from reliable sources in media or from market research firms.

After you've gotten hold of statistics related to your products or services' market, you can evaluate of your business in terms of the growth of its market. Let's say that your market has been growing at an annual average of 20% and your business's average annual growth rate is only 10%. This means that despite your "growing" numbers, you're actually losing market share. This also means that demand for your products or services is dwindling given the overall market perspective.

Another way to estimate market demand for your products or services is using what is known as a bottom-up approach. Under this perspective, you will need to draw certain assumptions that are supported with sound estimates, rationale and calculations.

Using the bottom-up approach, you will first need to ask the question of who will be your first 5, 50, 500 and 5,000 customers. Sound business planning and marketing activities require that you, as project manager, are able to understand your products or services' markets and prospects as intimately as possible and are able to test your products and services before marketing or promoting them to the public. Estimating your market demand must be done as precisely as can be done at every level.

Sound business planning requires that you're able to identify the first 5 prospects or customers that will patronize your new product or service and why they will do so. Next, you will focus on the next 50 customers that you can identify through good analysis of the market and submarkets and meetings with your salespeople. The next 450 prospects can be identified by segmenting the submarkets and the final 5,000 prospects can be inferred from the market demand that you'll be able to assess.

And after you've finished estimating market demand using this bottom-up perspective, it's better if you can evaluate this side-by-side with the earlier top-down approach in order to check for consistency.

Part of estimating market demand is understanding that each and every market for your product or service has a ceiling and floor, i.e., a maximum and minimum level. It is important to be aware of this because these can assist you in determining whether or not a new product or service is economically feasible. And for you to better understand this, you must be aware of the following market demand parameters:

- Total volume of divine potential customers.

- Limitations based on geographic locations.

- Total time to utilize a product or service.

Keep in mind that total market demand isn't fixed but is expressed as a function of certain established and assumed conditions. This function is dependent on several factors like economical, environmental and other market-related forces. And from there, the demand for your product or services can be estimated or defined. This demand is your company or group's estimated market share at different levels of marketing activities for a given time frame.

Forecasting Future Market Demand

History is filled with company and industry stories wherein fatal strategic errors were committed simply because of inaccurate estimation of demand. While many of these businesses and industries didn't lack in terms of highly scientific methodologies as they used historical trends smoothing, regression analysis and other equally valid statistical methods of analysis, their estimates were wrong because of a flawed fundamental assumption: relationships that affect market demand is static, i.e., unchanging. In short, many companies and industries we're blindsided by changes in the behavior of their end-users and by their respective markets' saturation points. And while there is a popular saying that history repeats itself, these failed companies and industries learned the hard way that this saying can't be taken as gospel truth, especially now that markets have become more global, more high tech, and more volatile.

It is because of changes in the market such as these that have led many project managers to distrust many traditional estimation techniques. In fact, some have even gone to the extreme by totally giving up on forecasting demand and simply plan their projects or businesses without the benefit of good market demand estimates. This however, is wrong. It may be impossible to perfectly assess market demand or anticipate possible changes in them but it is still possible to gain valuably deep insights as to your products or services' future market demand and conditions simply by gaining a deeper understanding of the dynamics and relationships that work it. And believe me, these insights can oftentimes be the thin line that separates a floundering project management strategy from a winning one.

While an estimate of your product or service's demand isn't in and by itself a guarantee for success, ditching it altogether will subject your projects to erroneous assumptions about market demand for your products or services. Explicitly gauging your products' or services' total market demand gives you a much higher chance of influencing your projects' successes. For your team, even just going through the process can be beneficial because your members will be compelled to really evaluate and rethink the market and your competitors instead of simply coming out with poorly thought of targets, numbers and answers.

Forecasting total market demand is only the first part of developing a winning project management strategy. As soon as you come up with an estimate of market demand, you're still not done with planning for your project.

In estimating or forecasting your products or services' total market demand, there are four steps you'll need to take.

Market Definition

First, you will need to define the market. At the beginning, you're better off being overly inclusive when it comes to defining your products or services' market instead of being under inclusive. IIere, you must be able to define your market broadly enough so that it includes all prospects and potential users in order for you to reduce the risk of being edged out by product or service substitutes as well as identify factors that can affect the demand for your products or services. Keep in mind that the driving factors for total market size forecasts or estimates are different from those that drive your particular product or service's market or category share.

A good example of this would be office telecommunications products. The total national market demand for these are partly dependent on the number of office workers in the country, their needs and their habits. The total demand for a particular type of office telecommunications product like PBX systems are dependent on their benefits vis-à-vis the other substitute products as well as their prices. Beyond this, the market demand for a specific type of PBX system is dependent on its benefits and price vis-à-vis its competitors.

When trying to define your market, you need understand the importance of available product substitutes. Keep in mind that your customers or prospects' behaviors may change if and when the performance or prices of potential substitutes for your products or services change as well. For example, a company that is studying market demand for commercial paper tubes has to take into consideration other uses of plastic and metal tubes that are highly related to their commercial paper tubes in order to minimize the risk of their customers switching to those product substitutes.

You also have to keep in mind that there is a risk that a

totally new product can take over the market of an existing one that seems to have comprised an entire market, as when the electronic calculator totally eliminated the use of slide rules. Another good example would be cellular phones. Its birth, growth and evolution have totally wiped out the telecommunications industry formerly known as pagers.

And there are different ways that you can ensure that you're able to take into consideration current and potential product or service substitutes. You can learn about product substitutes by interviewing industrial customers, learning from them about changes in the usage patterns of certain products that can give you insights as to whether or not switching opportunities are available for your customers. Doing market research and interviewing industry experts can also give you valuable insights as to recent developments that can either fortify your market share or erode it.

Lastly, you can gain great insights into your customers or prospects' potential to switch to product substitutes through careful quantification of such products' economic value to said customers or prospects. For example, you can ask yourself how changes in the prices of oil products may affect the prices of plastics, which in turn can significantly affect the ability of plastic products to substitute for paper or metal.

Analyzing these things can help you create a demand curve for your particular industry, i.e., graphs that present how price and volume for your products and services are related.

With appropriate market definitions, the demand curve for the industry is often times less steep than those for its component products or services. What this means is that the demand for the total industry is less sensitive to changes in market factors compared to the demand for the individual products that make up the total industry. A good example for this is the price of gasoline. Consumers of Gasoline A will simply switch to other brands if its price goes up and they're unlikely to stop buying gasoline should the prices of gasoline, as a whole, increase.

There are cases that you, as a project manager, can quickly make certain assumptions or judgments concerning your definition of the market. And there are cases too where you'll need to give considerable analysis and thought to your market. You need not make a total market forecast for your business strategy if defining the market will be very impractical or impossible and if your products or services have a very small share of the market. What will be your main challenge instead is to understand the competitiveness of your own products or services vis-a-vis the available substitutes for them.

Breaking Down Demand

The next step when forecasting market demand is breaking down total demand into its core components for individual analysis. Keep in mind that there are two criteria for choosing segments. First, ensure that your categories are standardized and small enough in order for your identified demand drivers to consistently work across the various components. Next, ensure that each category is also large enough to make all and of your analysis worth it. This is where your judgment comes into play.

It may help you as Product Manager to think of alternative segmentations , which may be based on different groups of users, say according to purchase types like for home use or industrial use. Then, formulate theories about what drives their demand for a particular product or service and decide how detailed should your analysis will be in order for your theories or analysis to be as realistic as possible. While continuing the assessment, you can refer back to this particular stage to evaluate whether or not your initial decisions are still valid.

For this, you can choose to use a tree diagram where the branches can represent different categories. Some of your categories may contribute greatly to overall demand while others won't. Some can also be fairly large or too diverse for any significant analysis to be done.

When considering market segments, you as a project manager must decide whether or not to utilize data that you already have or access to or to just commission another firm or person to do research for an independent estimate. In the United States, the Federal Government, industry associations, ongoing market data services or off-the-shelf studies conducted by industry experts may be considered reliable sources of public information on historical and segmented demand for many industries. For foreign markets or those that are less researched in the US, you may need to get the services of firms that specialize in independent estimates.

But even with good sources of data, it may be challenging to divide the information according to the most optimal categories for a meaningful analysis. In such cases, you as a project manager should decide if you'll conduct your own market research program - which can be expensive and time consuming - or simply forecast the market demand based on the available data that you already have.

Keep in mind that while breaking down into segments can help you estimate or forecast total demand, it may not be enough to help you create the necessary categories to develop a good marketing strategy. This is because a single product or service may have an entirely different set of factors that drive the demand for it. In this regard, consumer industry categories can be especially helpful when projecting the demand for the whole market but can be quite limited in terms of developing customer preference-based strategies, where such preferences are identified based on price, quality, service or based on other associated benefits. These particular categories or factors normally don't correlate with the same categories used in customer industry forecasting. But if you have a strong sales force, this shouldn't be a problem.

Demand Drivers Forecasting

The next important step is to understand what drives the demand for products or services in each of the categories you have identified and forecast such drivers. In this part, you can employ several good statistical techniques, such as regression, so you can establish relationships between historical demand and identified drivers of such. This however, is only the start. The more challenging part is looking beyond your data to see you which particular regressions are easily identified with other factors whose data can be especially challenging to collect. Afterwards, you need to take a prospective about how these other factors can evolve in the future.

Sensitivity Analysis

As a project manager, you're at higher risk if you only rely on demand forecasts based on a single point or factor. This is because some of your forecasts' macroeconomic variables may be wrong. And even despite your best analysis, other assumptions behind other drivers of demand can also be wrong. You must be able to ask yourself questions such as "What can cause forecasts to dramatically change?" in order to get the best estimates. Doing so can help you increase your chances of successfully identifying potential risks and stoppages that may be caused by developments in other technologies, competition in your industry and in costs of your suppliers. So after you have developed a baseline forecast, the next challenge is to know whether or not it is on target or off. And if its off-target, how far could it be.

At a certain level, sensitivity analysis can be done simply by changing your assumptions and putting a number on their impact on demand. But for a much better insight, you'd be better off using a more targeted approach.

Start your sensitivity analysis by pondering on and quantifying the areas of such forecast with the biggest or highest strategy risk. Your decision as to what strategy to use may be affected only if the forecasted demand is significantly less than your baseline forecast. In other cases, you may be subject to greater risks from small errors in your forecast.

Afterwards, estimate the chances for such developments. You may for example, compare your baseline forecast to actual, historical industry performance to see whether or not your forecast may be on or off-target.

Decide On the Best Approach

The forecasting approach you just read can work for simple assessments and comprehensive ones but you can use them in different ways to determine or forecast future market demand. As with some of the other ways of conducting market analysis, gauging the appropriate effort for your projects goals and objectives can be a significant challenge for demand forecasting. You should ask yourself: How much information should I have in order to decide?

As a project manager, it's not improbable for you to spend a lot of time conducting such an analysis. Some organizations have dedicated departments who work all year round on them. It goes without saying that the more time-consuming and through an analysis is, the higher the confidence will be in such analysis' results. And as such, you can exert the commensurate effort, which can significantly affect the choice for a project implementation strategy.

The usual case however is that time is limited, the issues at hand aren't complicated, or the forecasted total demand may not be significant enough to warrant certain levels of commitment. If such is the case, you as a project manager must quickly and inexpensively proceed. You can do so simply by relying on expert opinions and judgments or less-sophisticated statistical tools to forecast demand based on certain factors. Even such limited approaches can give you meaningful insights and is much better than having none at all. By getting the ball rolling on analyzing and forecasting demand, you as a project manager can figure out whether there are important issues concerning demand that need to be further analyzed.

Forecasting total demand can be very important when it comes to deciding on your project management strategies. Developing your independent forecasts using the approach I've outlined can help you get better insights and build better consensus and conviction to take action within your team through a good understanding of what drives the demand for your product or service as well as the risks involved in your forecasts.

Just keep in mind that there will always be uncertainties regardless of the soundness of your work. This is because stoppages or other curve balls are very hard to predict, particularly if these are caused by significant technological, macroeconomic or political developments. But if you as a project manager do the effort of analyzing or forecasting future market demand using this framework, you have a much higher chance of being able to spot or identify these risks compared to those who don't. And as such, you can make much better decisions for managing your projects effectively and successfully.

Chapter 3: How a Good Manager Plans a Project

Can you do any planning if you are not a professional planner? Of course, you can! Everyone does. When you decide that you are going to leave a certain hour of the day free so that you can watch a certain TV program, you have effectively made a plan. When you compile a list of ingredients to prepare for dinner, it is planning too. In fact, you need to take planning as a natural process – one you undertake because it is essential and necessary for the success of your day, your week, your year... generally your life.

Actually when you plan, you feel more reassured that you are going to implement that which you so desire. But without planning, you often keep on expressing your desire to do something but you keep postponing the actual implementation. It is on this basis that Antoine de Saint-Exupery, a Frenchman who wore many hats in the first half of the 20th century, from writer and poet to an aviator, declared that when you have a goal but no plan that goal remains a mere wish.

Key considerations for planning your projects

Objectives and Constraints

It has been said many times that failing to plan is the same as planning to fail. To ensure successful projects, you need to have a plan. A project plan clearly identifies how you intend to achieve the objectives of your project.

Objectives are the most important part of your project plans and these objectives need to be defined and clear in ways that they can be used to make your effective project plan. Objectives that are unclear or vague is akin to telling a cab driver to take you to New York City: its too vague and general to get you where you need to be exactly. When you define your objectives in a way that they can be useful in coming up with a good project plan is like asking the same cab driver, who is assumed to be an American, to take you to a specific New York City address while speaking in clear English – it allows the driver to map out the most efficient route to get you where you really need to be, which is your objective.

Objectives can be stated in different ways like:

- Scope, like the number of products, equipment needed or market reach.

- Technical, like the number of units produced, delivery time or the maximum frequency of defective product.

- Timing, such as project completion dates, system implementation needs or operational timelines.

- Budget, such as per unit cost of production, distribution costs or total project cost.

Identifying potential constraints that can limit your team's ability to achieve objectives is a natural part of defining your projects' objectives. Resources are unlimited and free only in a perfect world but unfortunately, your team and your project are operating in an imperfect one. As such, it's part of reality in dealing with constraints, regardless if you like it or not. The most common constraints that your projects will face include technology, cultural, financial, personnel and time constraints.

Stakeholders

Once you have identified your project's objectives as well as its constraints, you'll need to identify the parties that can be affected by or are involved in your project. You can do so by asking yourself who can benefit from it, who needs to participate to achieve its objectives, and who can be inconvenienced by it. And the most important people to identify are those who depend primarily on the success of your project. If you want your project succeed, it is imperative that you get the full and unwavering support of all your project's stakeholders. Simply put, no support equals no success.

Evaluating if your planned project is aligned with or related to the success of other units within your organization is one good way to elicit such support from stakeholders. If it isn't aligned or related, it may cause inevitable strain on your organization's resources, which can affect the successes of both the other units and your planned project. If some or all of your stakeholders know that the planned project won't benefit them, chances are you won't be able to get their support. Without their support, chances are you won't get your superiors' as well. Lack of support can significantly reduce your ability to complete projects successfully.

Strategy

After identifying your objectives as well the constraints, you can now come up with your strategy for successfully completing your project. Basically, your strategies outline how you will achieve the objectives you set for your project given the identified constraints. Strategies are bigger picture plans, much like a general map of California.

Keep in mind that coming up with your project's strategies

isn't as simple as merely conjuring action plans for achieving the objectives. It's more than that. Plans of action need to have some indicators or proven track records of a high success rate before you even consider them. If not, you're lowering your chances for successfully implementing your project, achieving their objectives and may even result in more problems than what you originally planned for. I'd like to take as an example, my niece Abigail.

Years ago, she had a really bad toothache. The plan of action that she chose is one that's universally accepted by many ignorant people as a good one, which is to just wait for it to subside. She thought that her toothache is the same as the many boys who were smitten by her beauty when she was still young – that they'd eventually go away when ignored long enough.

Her objective was very clear, which was to relieve herself of the pain caused by her tooth. She also had a seemingly good plan, which is to ignore it so it will go away. But that strategy is obviously very flawed but she committed herself to her strategy, bearing with all the pain and sticking to her, pardon the pun, gums. But after a while, her left cheek appeared to be as if she had mumps or so much food in her mouth, i.e., swollen. Her and usually bad smelling breath smelled even more putrid. And the reason for it was that it wasn't just an ordinary toothache. Turns out it was a really bad case of bacterial gum infection.

Because of her strategy to just leave it be, her lower left gums have become swollen – full of pus. If she had chosen a much better strategy, say going to the dentist, the root cause of her problem would have been easily identified and the right strategy, one that has a proven track record of success, could have been chosen: medicines. As such, she and her loved ones suffered the painful and, pardon the pun again, putrid consequences.

Identifying key issues, opportunities and threats are an integral part of coming up with your projects' strategy because these factors can potentially make it easier - or harder – for your projects to succeed. Going back to my niece's putrid example, she could've had an idea already that it wasn't just a simple toothache but a bacterial infection, given her unusually worse smelling breath. That could've been an indication to her that the toothache was more than that and as such, she could have easily neutralized the threat of her gums swelling like crazy. She could've taken the necessary medicines and nipped the problem at the bud. But because of her failure to properly assess the risk or threat, she was blindsided by it when it materialized in the form of swollen, pus filled and painful gums.

The same goes for our planned projects. You need to correctly identify the issues, threats and opportunities that can either spell success or failure even before coming up with your project management strategies.

Your Team

Now that you've identified your objectives, constraints, issues, threats and opportunities as well as having devised a project management strategy, you can now organize your team for the project. Basically, you'll be recruiting a group of people who will be responsible for implementing your project's plans and strategies. Projects can be completed one way or the other even if the plan isn't sensible for as long as you have the right people for the team. On the other hand, a sensible plan without the right people will fail. An expert in the subject of management said that his company's greatest resource are his people. It should be the same for your projects.

Putting together a competent team is not a simple as getting your usual supplies from the grocery. It involves some mental effort, particularly for figuring out who will be the best fit for certain tasks and responsibilities involved in the project as well as making them want to do their jobs well. You can think of assembling a competent team for your project as preparing a roast turkey for thanksgiving. You don't just get the first turkey that you lay your eyes on at the grocery store, but you pick the best possible turkey for dinner. If after inviting your boss over for Thanksgiving dinner, would you even consider getting the cheapest and worst quality turkey for the occasion? I don't think so, especially if a good part of your plan for inviting your boss over for Thanksgiving dinner is to "encourage" him or her into raising your pay or promoting you. If you're that careful when hosting a thanksgiving dinner with your boss as guest, you should take the same care in your approach to organizing your project team.

Once we have identified our objectives, constraints, opportunities, threats and issues and have devised a strategy, we then organize the project team, i.e., the group of people who will be implementing the planned project based on the strategy we have devised. When a project has no sensible plan but have the right people, it will be completed one way or the other. Something gets done however rightly or wrongly. But a sensible plan without the right people will either go nowhere or fail miserably. Some expert management guru once said that people are his company's greatest resource. Well, it's our projects' too.

Assembling the team is not as simple as picking apples from a tree. It requires some mental exercise too, particularly checking for those that are best fit for certain activities of the project and making them want to do their parts well. Think of it as preparing to bake an apple pie. You don't just pick apples from the grocery shelf. You pick the best apples possible. Will you go for rotten apples for that sumptuous apple pie you plan to give to your boss to cajole him or her into promoting you? I don't think so. So it is with organizing our project team.

So how do you go about planning in order to achieve your goal?

Be realistic about what you want.

You see, the reason you can't begin to defreeze the chicken when you are going to eat out at dinner time is because that isn't normal; doesn't make sense. By the same token, you need not look at project planning from an academic point of view. To succeed, you need to engage in activities that are relevant to your project; take actions that will advance your process towards achieving your goal. Take a natural approach to your planning and you'll have your track well covered.

Highlight your objective

Here you want to have a general direction of where you want your project to be within a given period. Before you begin taking action, it is good that you break the whole thing down into different segments. Each segment will contain the important actions you need to take before you can declare the segment well done.

A good example is when you decide to have a project in the name of annual holiday. Don't you need to know when it is due? And once you are certain of the timing you also need to decide the place you want to visit. Once that is done, it is imperative that you break down your project into segments for ease of implementation. In our example here, you may have ticket booking as an important segment where you decide the airline to use, the hotel to reside in, the timing of your flight... all that. Then you could have another segment on packing where you decide what items to take with you on your trip, size of your luggage and so on.

Make your project end the starting point

What this essentially means is that in order to make a good plan, you need to keep focus on where you want to be at the end; and that is from the onset. For instance, if you want to fly out at the end of the month and it is mid-month now, you can tell that you only have two weeks to plan for your trip. If you want to take some items with you and you don't have them now, you have got to think about how long it is going to take for the supplier to deliver those items to you.

And in that light, you may decide to put the task of ordering for those items before the task of booking your flight or even that of packing your items. In fact, in your planning, packing could be the last task in your list of things to do. In short, for effective planning, work backwards. That way, you are able to organize your timing logically, taking into account the tasks that are dependent on others. You, certainly, don't want a situation where you are handling a housing project, for instance, and your painters set base before wall plastering has been done! If that happens, you'll have a lot of downtime, with painters setting camp to wait for the appropriate time to do their bit. And what a waste that would be!

Do reasonable evaluation of the project cost

What happens when you bite more than you can chew? Well, you are bound to suffer in more ways than one; and that includes having what many governments suffer from – proliferation of white elephants! That means you pour resources in a badly planned project and your resources get depleted long before your project is completed; so it stalls – or it is completed but ends up being unusable due to high maintenance costs. Even if at this stage you are working with estimates, let them be realistic.

Break down your project

What you need to do now is to break down your entire project into stages so that you know what to start with, what to follow, and so on, till the project is completed.

Here are some questions that will help you to determine how to plan your project stages:

- Exactly what do I need to do?

- If it's the buying of an air ticket; booking a hotel; prior shopping; you need to note down each of those tasks.

- What is my budget?

- This is important because you need to gauge it against, say, the cost of living in your holiday destination; the length of your holiday; and so on.

- Who is the best person to carry out what task?

- Allocating tasks to people as per their competence and overall diligence is very important. You need to use people that you can trust to do their jobs well. You also need to spell out each task clearly to the person in-charge of it.

- Are the people I want for individual tasks available at the time I need them?

- The point is you need to be on the same page with everyone concerned if you are going to succeed in your project. In an organization, for instance, it would be disastrous for you to handpick individuals for your project without having a conversation with their respective department heads or line managers.

- How will I know when each task is completed?

- You need to have a verification process. For instance, you need to agree with everyone involved how you are going to get their feedback. If it is by e-mail, for instance, the point needs to be well understood. Without proper communication, you may think that tasks are on schedule, when, in actual fact, someone has encountered a problem. Yet you would need to come to the rescue so that the project timing is not derailed.

If you go about planning your project in the way explained in this chapter, you will find the execution stage relatively easy to handle. In addition, your project management will not be as difficult as some people take it to be. Actually, with proper project planning, you end up accomplishing a lot and enjoy your experience at the same time. It is very motivating to find yourself moving forward with every move, just because you have everything well laid out, knowing what to anticipate at every stage of the project.

Chapter 4: More Tips On How To Plan Projects Well

You've learned much about how a good manager plans a project in Chapter 3. And if you want to up the ante even further, here are some more pieces of advice on planning your projets well.

Allow your team members to choose their tools

Granted when it comes to technology you can determine the level of automation or otherwise that you want for the implementation of your project, but when it comes to details, say what shape or color of the tools to be used for various tasks, let the people who are meant to use the tools have a say. You don't, for instance, have to be too harsh because a team member wants to do his or her analysis using excel when your organization is still stuck in the Lotus spreadsheets.

And when it comes to any change of course, let the affected members of your team be in the loop. It is demoralizing for an employee, for example, to wake up one morning eager and already set to perform a certain task that was on the schedule from the onset, only for you to declare that the task has been cancelled or re-scheduled. You are not just disorienting the employee for the rest of the day if you do that; it also makes the employee feel alienated. The long and short of this advice is to endeavor to communicate effectively with everyone involved in the project and have a discussion on the details so that you settle on what the people on the ground are comfortable with.

Avoid basing your decisions on the limitations that you see

As a project manager, you are just a single mind. Much as you are in the team leader's seat, you need not assume that just because your project tools can only perform this much that is all that should be attempted. If you do that, you will be inhibiting the creativity of individual team members. It is advisable, instead, to tell your team members what you aim to achieve, as you show them the tools and resources available. You may be surprised at their genius. If a team member chooses to use one tool for more than one task and it works, well and good. As a project manager, you need to be flexible, accommodating and supportive. That way, not only do you minimize or even avoid conflict within your team, you also make the working environment conducive for everyone – which allows people to think outside the box and accomplish what may have seemed insurmountable.

Make your communication effective

You are in charge of the project and you know what it entails. So no-one is going to dictate any particular mode of communication for you. However, whether you choose to have your team to meet every morning to review the previous day's work and discuss the day's tasks – the way it happens in scrum – or you base your communication on some tools of group project management, it does not matter. What is important is that you adopt a communication method that ensures that everyone is on the same page at every stage of the project. Information should be communicated in a timely fashion particularly when it comes to change of plans. Effective communication strengthens a team and you need a strong team to succeed in your project. So communicate well and regularly.

Provide for plan adjustments

So you want to be efficient? Well, allocating a task for every minute of your day is not the way to go. Suppose one of your painters in a building project trips and pours the gallon of paint? Won't you need some spare minutes to send someone back to the store to bring a fresh gallon of paint? If you have overstretched yourself and everyone else involved in the project, people are likely to feel stressed or get into panic mode whenever something goes amiss, no matter how minute. When people know that there is no breathing space left, they are likely to be on edge as they work. As such they approach the project tasks as if they are very complex and they tend to feel deficient. That is why it is advisable to leave enough room for adjusting the plan for the day if need be.

Make room for eventualities

You surely cannot be so rigid that you can't change the color of your iron sheets, for instance, if you find that there is a wholesaler who is clearing his stock and selling it for half the normal price, only that he doesn't have the color you have in your project plan. Is this not an opportunity to make much needed savings in your project? After all, the color of iron sheets is not like the gauge – it has nothing to do with quality; just superficial.

And just as you need to be prepared to seize business opportunities when they crop up, so should you be prepared to handle hitches when you encounter them. For example, a gardening wedding doesn't stop just because rain has fallen from nowhere in an otherwise hot season. There are tents that you can use and there are halls that people can shift to – you just need to be prepared to accommodate such eventualities.

Encourage light moments

All work without... Yes, you need to relax and get time to rejuvenate – it's not just about avoiding to look dull but also about avoiding burn out. What's the big deal, for instance, if one of you had 'the best formula' away from the books but ended up with ridiculous results on that particular segment of the project? It's actually healthy to laugh at the apparent know-it-all attitude that the person may have shown, because nobody gets tense and no egos are injured.

In the meantime, you all get to learn that it is not for nothing that procedures are laid down; that it is prudent to follow the laid down procedures and work as per the plan unless the conditions have become untenable. Many successful business owners have made mistakes, admitted them and learnt from them. The world doesn't turn upside down just because the way you tackled a challenge did not help matters – but you get to sharpen your project management skills from such experiences.

Chapter 5: Common Reasons For Failed Projects

Why is it important to learn about project execution when you already have a good plan in place? Well, a good plan is good to look at, of course, and to imagine you working with it, but in the context of running a project, the plan is as good as its implementers. If they know how to implement the actions laid down in the plan in the prescribed manner, leaving room for adjustments as necessary, then you are fine. However, if the project manager is a poor leader or is even egoistic, even the good plan can't make your project successful.

You need to know what not to do as a project manager. In short, once you know the main weaknesses that make a project fail, you will be conscious of them as you carry out your project, and you can then avoid falling victim. Various studies conducted by the Project Management Institute and institutions like Carnegie Mellon University contain the following as major causes of project failure:

Objectives being vague or poorly defined

If surely it is not clear where you want your project to look like at various stages, how would you know whether you are on the right track? When clarity of direction lacks, you only get to realize that your end result is unsatisfactory when it is too late to make corrections.

Shaky project sponsorship

If you are going to succeed in your project, you had better be certain that the funds you have planned for are available as and when you need to use them. Otherwise your project could delay or even fail.

Poor leadership

You may not be a very social person, but if you take up the role of project manager, it is important that you make an effort to keep your communication channels open. You need to be approachable otherwise people in your team will not speak out when they encounter problems until you unravel the challenges they are facing – somctimes when it is too late.

Having a project manager without relevant skills

How far do you think your flock of sheep can advance if the lead sheep is limping? Similarly, if the project manager is poorly trained and has no experience to cover for the lack in training, then the project cannot go well.

Poorly covered scope

If you become impulsive during the execution of your project instead of following your set plan, you could find your team performing some great tasks but which are outside the scope of your project. And, of course, anything that is irrelevant is unhelpful as far as your particular project is concerned.

Poor handling of changes

If you have to make some changes – structural or otherwise – during some stage in your project, how everyone in the team handles it is very important. You want to have your team pulling together towards the same cause even when it has become necessary to deviate a bit from the original plan.

Poor definition of project requirements

If you quote your supplies in general terms, for instance, who is to say that you aren't going to get sizes that don't fit; quality that is below par; and so on? Only when you make your specifications clear can you be sure that all stakeholders keep to plan. And the same case applies to requirements like timing. Your team will strive to keep a timeline is it is clearly stated; if not, the project gets delayed and you end up incurring unplanned costs.

Failure to consult with other stakeholders

Project management is not a one-person show. If you behave like it is, just because you are the project manager, chances are that you are going to risk being sabotaged by your team members or others concerned. If, for example, you do not consult with senior management where funding is concerned, how are you going to execute your project to conclusion if management does not approve certain payments?

Failing to put a plan in place to handle risks

Do you think you are going to face a catastrophe during the life of your project? Well... Is it really possible to tell? Actually, it's not. Otherwise if you did know some danger was going to come, you would avoid it by all means. However, you have room to provide for unforeseen challenges by keeping some money aside to spend on handling unforeseen problems; hiring external personnel; and so on.

Having an unrealistic budget

If you understate your project budget just so that management can approve its funding, it will be like shooting yourself in the foot. The same people are the ones you are going to find when seeking additional funding and you are bound to have a problem explaining that you have not squandered your initial vote.

Now – those are some of the weaknesses that make projects fail. What can you specifically do to increase your chances of project success?

Chapter 6: Complete Your Projects Successfully!

Knowing what not to do is only just a portion of successfully completing your projects. More than knowing which mistakes to avoid, you must know what exactly to do to ensure successfully completed projects. In this chapter, you'll learn how to enjoy successful projects.

Identify a good project sponsor

When you are considering a good sponsor, think in terms of someone who commands respect within your organization. You want someone who can influence individual team members to get committed because of his or her own level of commitment – someone inspiring. You also want a person who has the management's ear or whom management respects. This is because every now and then the project team is going to need some assistance from the management and their co-operation is crucial to the success of the project.

Design a communication plan

This communication plan is between you and all other project stakeholders. If you think about it, which is the lesser evil – having a supplier fail to make deliveries in good time or team members failing to show up for the day? Surely, both of these scenarios are detrimental to the success of your operations. To avoid such frustrating and potentially risky scenarios, it is advisable that you have a good plan on how to share ideas, expectations, and other foreseeable challenges amongst all project stakeholders. That way every person will feel personally responsible for the success of the project.

Spell out the project's measure of success

When everyone knows the indicators you are going to use, as a team, as the success scale, they feel motivated; having a mark to work towards. Besides, when you mention that standards have not been met at a certain stage of the project, everyone can see that you are saying that objectively – there being a measure set and spelt out in advance. With this kind of scale known and being communicated to everyone at the beginning of the project, you find yourselves speaking along the same wavelength; so misunderstandings are minimized, if not altogether avoided.

Lay out the methodology to follow in advance

It is important that everyone involved in the project knows

the methodology you intend to use for your project and understand it as well. And everyone in the team needs to understand the phases the project is scheduled to go through and what every phase entails. They need to know the key points to note in every phase in order to make every phase successful. And, of course, everyone involved needs to understand the expected end results, not just at the end of every phase but also at the end of the project.

Let your project have a clear schedule

For any plant project, schedules are very important. It's impossible to assign resources effectively and efficiently - manpower or material - without proper scheduling of work. without it, it would also be very challenging to manage your project cash flows and consequently, complete your projects according to your time line.

If you know that from Point A the next stage is, automatically, Point B, anxiety doesn't build amongst the team members. Likewise, if you know that you must sequentially skip one point and have an A-C-E-G kind of sequence, well and good. The important thing is that you know what to expect as you move along with the project, the various timings and so on. You also need to know who is involved in what task so you can tell whom to liaise with in different matters. All these factors need to be communicated to everyone and kept alive in their minds through regular communication. And you need to keep the project sponsor in the loop too.

We'll talk about project scheduling in more detail in Chapter 4

Manage resources well

It goes without saying that you won't be able to complete your project successfully without the necessary resources. But having them isn't the guarantee for success. It's because if you don't manage what you have very well, you still may not be able to successfully complete your project. But if you handle them well, you can still successfully complete your project even if there's not enough of it.

To make it easier for you, you can use a project management software that feature components that are models for resource management. After identifying and assigning whatever available resources you have the key activities in your project, such a software will come up with an efficient resource - loading plan, but you can Tweet as the project proceeds based on among other things, time constraints and resource availability.

Leveling of resources. Leveling of resources is a method for managing projects where you determine the starting and finishing dates and adjust them accordingly based on constraints on available resources. This is done. this is done so that you can balance the supply and demand for each of your project resources.

You can do resource leveling when for example, when you're trying to schedule several projects simultaneously but there is a shortage in resources like labor, which may be needed by other projects as well. Where the resource leveling, you can schedule the project in such a way that the available resources can be adequate for completing all of the project activities.

Let's say you're managing a project that requires the complete restoration of 3 classic cars. Further, let's assume that there's only 1 painter and 1 paint gun for your project. You can use resource leveling to schedule activities of the project in such a way that the project can be completed even with just one painter and paint gun.

For example, you can prioritize the car that requires the most effort in terms of repainting and then painting the car that's simplest to finish last. Painting cars, especially if it involves a total restoration, requires several layers of paint. So after you're done painting the basic primer coating of the first car, you can work on the 2nd and then on the 3rd as you wait for the primer of the first car to dry completely. And while you're waiting for the primer coatings of the 2nd and the 3rd automobiles to dry, you can start painting the second layer on the first car and so on.

Resource management software programs allow you to estimate potential delays in your projects and also helps you automatically update the subsequent activities' schedules in accordance with such delays. Such programs put off or delay tasks or activities until the prerequisite ones or the necessary resources become available.

You can use resource management software programs to smooth out your resource leveling activities in two ways: time-constrained and resource-constrained scheduling. When you schedule your project's activities based on time constraints, the use of resources is the one that will be adjusted in accordance with time constraints. On the other hand, the deadlines or the activities' duration will be adjusted according to constraints in resources when a resource-constrained scheduling is used.

Basic practices for allocating resources

Identifying what work or activities need to be done for the project is the first thing that you should do when allocating resources. And for this, critical path method or CPM software programs can help you much. If you're not able to identify the needed worker activities for your projects, there's nothing for you to allocate your resources to.

The next step is for you to identify and list all your available resources in the form of a resource inventory. Such an inventory may include basic information about the resources, their names, their schedules or availability, among other important details. And after you've created the inventory, you can proceed with assigning them to specific tasks or activities that require them. And after deploying your resources, you can evaluate the current need for such resources by classifying such needs according to the type of resources as well as your project activities' time periods.

Lastly, you can reallocate or adjust resources using CPM software, should the need to do so arise. Otherwise, just stick with your allocation and allow your project activities to run their natural courses.

Manage costs well

You can boost your projects' productivity in 3 ways: higher revenues, lower costs, or both. But what if your project isn't a revenue generating one and it's merely a cost center? How can your project help the organization as a whole improve profitability or how can its cost be acceptable for approval by upper management? In this case, your 3 options are immediately reduced to just one – cost reduction.

Managing costs is very crucial aspect of project management. Failure to keep costs under control can be the determinant as to whether or not your project can be completed successfully or remain unfinished. Managing or controlling your costs can help you answer important questions like how much to spend for your project, if your spending levels are normal or not, how to manage situations wherein your team overspends, how to best distribute your budget across the project's different activities and how to control costs in general. As the project manager, you'll need to prepare a detailed budget plan and schedule. You'll also need to have your projects' shareholders on board because their cooperation is vital.

Different project managers manage costs associated with their projects differently from one another. This is because each organization has different accounting and financial goals and objectives that may render standardized practices and standards ineffective or inefficient for achieving budgetary goals.

As an activity or process, cost management is composed of key activities like budget setting, planning, setting budgetary authorities, systematic analysis of actual costs, collecting important cost data for such analysis, implementation of corrective actions in the event the team exceeds the established budget, overall evaluation of actual spending on the project and giving recommendations, if any, after completion of projects.

Managing project costs also include elements such as activity-based accounting, project accounting, earned value analysis and breaking down of work structures. Activity-based accounting refers to cost recognition and budgeting that is based on certain activities or tasks that have already been pre-defined, which are more detailed than project accounting. On the other hand, project accounting simply refers to giving an accounting number or code to projects that have already been approved for a more accurate and easier way of allocating costs. Earned value analysis, also known as EVA, analyzes variances or differences in costs, i.e., how far are actual costs from budgeted ones. Lastly, breaking down work structures may be thought of as the "action" version of organizational charts that ranks particular tasks or activities in order of significance or importance instead of people and positions.

When talking about cost management, it's important to estimate costs well and keep actual ones down.

Estimating Costs

Your ability, as project manager, to keep your projects' costs as low as possible may be the single biggest difference that determines whether or not you'll be able to complete your project or just leave it hanging for eternity. The more accurate your cost estimates are, the higher the chances of your projects being successfully financed to completion.

Let's say that your organization can only afford to spend $200,000 for a project that can increase overall profitability by as much as 10% annually and that spending more than that will lead to reduced profitability instead. If you incorrectly estimate that $200,000 will be enough to successfully complete that project, which led you to complete only 80% of the project with the budget, your organization will need to borrow money or put in more money that could've been put to more profitable use just to finance the unfinished 20%. Either way, it will increase the organization's overall cost of capital and consequently, reduce overall profitability.

In the above-mentioned example, accurately estimating the project cost could've saved the organization money by not pushing through with the project and instead, could've allowed it to invest the money in more profitable ventures. This is why accurate estimates are valuable for the organization's profitability.

While it's true that no estimate is perfect or exact, some things can help you improve your cost estimating skills significantly for your planned projects. These include:

- Documentation: When you properly document your data collection activities, you can significantly improve your project cost estimates, according to the U.S. Government Accountability Office or US-GAO. This includes using current cost quotations to supplement the historical data you may have already gathered.

- Checking Out the Competition: While this may prove to be quite challenging, it can help you significantly improve your cost estimates' accuracy if done well. It's because you are able to access – and use real world data that's highly related to what you're planning for your projects. Compared to researching historical or estimated data on the costs of labor and materials for one of your planned projects, data on how much other organizations actually spent for both in order to successfully complete projects very much similar to what you have planned.

- Recording: Accurately and consistently keep records of your projects' detailed costs to help you improve your cost estimating ability for future planned projects via historical costing. And don't forget to provide enough leeway or allowance for the effects of inflation, i.e., price increases, over time.

Keeping Project Costs Down

It's absolutely essential for you to be able to keep your projects' costs down to successfully keep to within your projects' budgets and complete it successfully. Here are some ways that can help you do that consistently:

- Increase Spending: Yes, you're not hallucinating with this one. In a way, expensive can be the new cheap and always going for the cheapest can actually end up costing you more overall. Ok, let me explain using a personal example.

When I needed to buy a new LED TV, I had the option of going for the more popular brands like Samsung or Panasonic instead of the lesser-known brands that are significantly cheaper. Being one that's frugal and financially savvy, I chose to go with the cheaper brand of course. Guess what, less than 2 years after getting the TV, its motherboard broke down – just a few months after the 1-year warranty has already expired. After having 2 qualified technicians look at it, I was informed that the motherboard is irreparable and either I have it replaced, which can also cost a fortune or buy a new one. Either way, I'll end up spending more money.

Compare it to our other TV – an LCD one that was more expensive than the one that broke down. But guess what – it's still working fine after more than 4 years. And if I factor in the replacement of the motherboard, the higher priced TV that's still working after more than 4 years came out to be the real cheaper alternative.

When it comes to your projects, going for the cheapest equipment can lead to unwanted repair costs that can actually make your project more expensive and going for the cheapest people to make up your project team can do so as well with frequent mistakes or worse, incompetency. That's why in a sense, spending "more" makes sense in terms of keeping costs down.

Now I'm not saying that you should always gun for the most expensive items and manpower. I'm just saying that you shouldn't automatically go for the cheapest alternatives with hopes of keeping your costs as low as possible. Always consider the quality first and once you've established quality, go for the alternatives that can provide such quality at the lowest possible price, which will certainly be more expensive than the lower quality and cheapest alternatives.

- Details: One of the most common reasons for blowing project budgets is getting the wrong materials and people because of failure to pay attention to details. Either the project manager failed to notice the details of the materials or personnel acquired or he or she gave the wrong details to the suppliers. Even if you're able to rectify the mistakes without spending extra, the amount of time wasted simply to rectify mistakes and the delays they can cause can lead to higher project costs overall.

Risk management

Risk management is one of the hottest areas of the business world for the last 10 years or so, especially with what happened in the 2008 United States financial crises triggered by what was called sub-prime mortgages as well as the very prominent financial and accounting scandals that rocked some of the US' biggest firms like Enron and Long-Term Capital Management (LTCM). These event have made it clear that organizations need to have effective risk management systems in place if they're to survive in today's volatile and risky business environments.

In order to understand risk management well, you'll first need to define what risk is. Simply put, risk is the chance or probability of something undesirable happening. Crossing the street exposes you to risk of being road kill. Yes, there's a chance that you can get run over by a speeding vehicle. However, the habit of looking both ways before even crossing the street – even on a pedestrian lane – significantly reduces that risk because by seeing whether or not there are speeding vehicles approaching, you'll be able to cross the street only when there's no imminent danger from such vehicles.

It's the same with the projects that you manage. Whether you like it or not, there are a myriad number of ways that things can go wrong. Risks are everywhere and unfortunately, you can't eliminate risk. However, you can manage them well - just like in the above-mentioned example of crossing the street - so that the chances of things going wrong become very, very small and the chances of you successfully managing the project and achieving its objectives become much, much higher.

So what does it really mean to manage your project risks well? It means, among other things, that you can lower the chances of undesirable events becoming a reality. Another way of managing your project risks well is by minimizing the possible effects on your projects when those undesirable events do happen.

One of the most common ways that you can manage your projects' risks is through planning. Important project resources like buildings, warehouses and even vehicles can be destroyed fires, accidents and other calamities. While it is impossible to address and arrest all possible causes of fires, accidents and calamities, you can manage your projects' risks by planning – and implementing – steps to ensure that the chances of these happening are reduced significantly. Some of the ways you can do this is by prohibiting the storage of highly flammable materials inside the office, prohibiting smoking and installing high-quality circuit breakers that quickly trip and cut power off as soon as a major electrical short-circuit happens.

In terms of mitigating losses resulting from risks that do materialize, you can get insurance for your physical resources (property and equipment) as well as for your personnel. For physical resources, you can get fire insurance and comprehensive automobile insurance while for personnel, you can require key positions – especially those that handle cash – to be bonded up to a conservatively high amount. That way, if anything happens to your physical resources or one of your key personnel screws up or worse, defrauds the organization, you're at least assured of being monetarily compensated for any losses that may arise from them.

In managing your project risks, there are three steps you'll need to take: identification, quantification or measurement, and mitigation of your projects' risks.

Identify

You cannot quantify or even manage something that you are not aware of. This is why you'll need to first identify all the possible risks your projects may face. One of the easiest and simplest ways to do this is to simply ask yourself: What are the things that I don't want to happen while the project is ongoing? Chances are, answering that question will give you many ideas about the potential risks your projects may face.

All your projects may be subject to three types of risks: scope, schedule and resource risks. The chances of your estimates such as cost, budget, activity duration and resources needed being wrong are called scope risk. The probability that your projects may not be completed on time due to the inability to promptly complete their component activities is referred to as schedule risk. Lastly, the chances that your projects may suffer from a shortage in quantity or quality (or both) of needed resources for successfully completing them is called resource risk.

Quantify

If you'd like to get a very good grip on the risks your projects may face, it's best if you're able to express them in the numerical terms. Let's consider scope risk, which you can quantify by simulating variances in results. For example, you can simulate what can happen if your estimated cost is off by at least 25%, which means spending 25% more than your budget. If your original budget is $100,000, a 25% variance means overspending by as much as $25,000. You can toggle the numbers or potential variances to have an idea of just how much risks your projects are exposed to and up to what extent can it be tolerated.

Let's also consider schedule risk. You can express this in

dollar terms by estimating your projects' cost per unit of delay, e.g., per hour, per day or per week. These costs can come in the form of additional labor costs, lost opportunities to earn income and penalties incurred for not completing projects on schedule.

If for example, your daily labor cost for a project is $500 and you expect to generate at least $1,000 in daily revenues once the project has been completed, you can run a simulation to determine how much you stand to lose if the project is delayed by one week. In this scenario, you will incur additional labor cost of $3,000 - assuming a six-day workweek - and lost income opportunities amounting to $6,000 assuming the same. If you add it up, your quantified scheduled risk for a 1-week delay in the completion of your project is $9,000.

Mitigate

Now that you've qualified or estimated your projects' risks, you need to take the final step, which is to act on them by mitigating them. In my example earlier about crossing the street, looking both ways is one way of acting upon the risk of getting run over by speeding vehicle, thereby mitigating such risk. And if after looking both ways you see a speeding vehicle approaching, you can neutralize the risk by staying at the sidewalk and wait for the vehicle to pass before proceeding to cross.

For your projects, one of the best ways you can mitigate its risks is, as I mentioned earlier, getting insurance on the most critical aspects of your projects. And you know what, it isn't just business that are mitigating risks this way. Consider for example Jennifer Lopez, who insured her buttocks for $300 million. That's right, $300 million for her booty! While it may seem ludicrous for many of us mere mortals, it makes perfect business sense for her to do so because much of her fame - which is why she's so darn rich – is due to her behind. By ensuring them for such an amount, she is mitigating the risks of her finances being negatively affected by any accidents that can happen to her booty. Now if people like her can get insurance on, of all things, her buttocks, what more for your project's most important and critical resources?

Another way that you can mitigate your projects' risks is by refraining from always outbidding your competitors with dirt-cheap prices for projects. How does doing this help mitigate your risks? Bidding too low for projects tend to minimize your income from such. And the smaller your income from projects become, the less buffer you have to help mitigate risks from potential and unexpected increases in costs related to the projects awarded to you. When you bid higher than your absolute lowest, you give your team enough buffer or leeway in case the costs involved in completing your projects suddenly and significantly increase.

Finally, you can implement necessary controls as a way of mitigating your risks. These include dual control over important resources like cash and checks, approvals for project activities that require counter signing and strict implementation of rules, regulations and policies. And in **Chapter 5**, we'll talk about risk management in much greater detail.

Common Sense Risk Management

You may be managing projects that aren't as complicated as those of the big boys' and as such, you either don't have the budget for complex computer programs or the budget for such. The good news is that for most projects, common sense is a very feasible approach to project risk management.

Be wise with the changes you make

You are allowed to make changes in your project, of course, as long as you do not fundamentally deviate from the project's purpose. After all, you get wiser along the way, don't you? But not every change proposed by your team members should get your endorsement. You need to gauge each of them against the cost of the project; the impact it may have on the quality of output; and the overall impact on the project.

Avoid getting derailed by hiccups

Who denounces meals just because of some hiccups? Or

abandoned a journey because they happened to   a couple of times on their door front? Sometimes in the course of your project you encounter problems you didn't anticipate, but these should not discourage you from continuing with the project. If in the course of your road building project you encounter a water problem; one that your engineers didn't detect earlier on because it wasn't there and only occurred due to a recent natural phenomenon, think of ways to divert your route – get expert engineers to give you technical advice; government agencies for a quick regulatory resolution; anyone who can help fix the problem fast.

The important thing is to keep tabs on what is happening on your project on a consistent basis so that you can nip problems in the bud as they appear. And, of course, an important reminder – to have some contingency measures in place well factored in your project plan.

Have reasonable documentation

Is yours a writing project? If not, why for the sake of time management would you wish to have volumes and volumes of documentation that consume so much time that time spared for actual operations is constricted? You need to be realistically economical with every resource, including time. If your project is small, just have some basic guidelines and get on with business. And if your project is medium-sized, increase your paperwork commensurately; and so on.

Assess your performance

It isn't over till it's... True – you can't claim your project is done until you have confirmed that you have followed through with your initial plan. Here, it means you gauging the quality of work done against the standards set in your plan; checking your timing against your planned schedule; gauging your actual expenditure against your set budget; and everything else that you put down in your plan.

You should be able to tell how well you have succeeded in keeping to your plan (or how badly you have deviated from it) and also the much you have learnt – in specifics – from the challenges you encountered. And, of course, you don't declare the project completed before you have had a talk about it with the project sponsor and the main project stakeholders. You need to be on the same page when you declare it is officially over.

You can evaluate your projects in several ways – according to profitability, schedule and cost. For projects whose main purpose isn't profitability, like building your family's house, schedule and cost are the only relevant measures by which they're evaluated. The benchmarks or the minimum standard for evaluating such are spending no more than what was budgeted and finishing the projects no later than the scheduled or estimated completion date. Projects that have profitability as the primary objective, all 3 are the measures by which they'll be evaluated. It also has a 4th measure, which is target income is another criterion for evaluation. We'll take a look at how to evaluate project results in more detail in **Chapter 9**.

Compile critical feedback

Don't you want to be a better project manager next time around? Then seek to get genuine feedback from your team members, your project sponsor, and also the main project stakeholders. You need to know where they feel the project's strengths lay and where there were weaknesses. You can also benefit from hearing what they think you could have done better. Call it a form of all round informal appraisal. Such feedback can only make you a wiser, more confident project manager.

The points offered in this chapter are meant to help you manage your project better, with structured planning; use of appropriate tools; insightful project management; as well as great interpersonal skills.

Chapter 7: Project Scheduling

Without the benefit of a computer program, creating a very detailed schedule of activities for your projects can be quite challenging to say the least, especially when you need to change certain items or activities that require subsequent adjustments in others that are dependent on said items or activities. That being said, detailed project scheduling without the aid of computers or software may be too tedious to make the whole thing worth it.

And when it comes to using computers or software for detailed project scheduling, the simplest and best way to go about it is to use a CPM or Critical Path Model software. This can help you to easily identify activities that comprise the whole project, understand how they're related to each other and based on these, generate a detailed enough project activities schedule. Because using programs help you automatically adjust other variables in relation to those you have manually changed or modified, using computers and software can make it easy for you as project manager to conduct what-if scenario analysis for your projects. This is just one of the many benefits you can enjoy from using a CPM or other similar software for preparing detailed project schedules.

Critical Path Method (CPM)

Using this very, if not most, popular project scheduling method, you can:

- List the activities that need to be conducted to successfully complete your projects. The best way to go about this break down such activities according to phases or deliverables.

- Estimate the duration or time frame for each activity. The easiest way to do this is by estimating time frames for the completion of each activity and use such estimates as official duration for such activities. The different natures of each activity may result in different units of duration for each activity's time frame, e.g., in hours, days, or weeks.

You can also estimate duration in terms of effort. For example, stripping the paint of the body of a truck can take 3 painters 60 man-hours to finish, which means the average man-hours needed by each painter is 20 hours. The 20 hours then becomes the official estimate of task duration for stripping a truck's body off its paint, which is an expression of effort in numerical terms.

Another way of estimating this is by taking the longest time for finishing the job among the 3 painters. If painters 1, 2 and 3 finished their jobs in 19, 23 and 21 hours, respectively, the official estimated duration in terms of effort is 23 hours – the longest of the 3.

- Identify the activities' relationship with each other. Because the activities that comprise your projects will always have constraints, it may be affected by many other factors such as the successful completion of other activities, commitment dates, resource availability (or unavailability), various conditions and availability of labor.

- Set deadlines and time constraints. Finish No Later Than (FNLT) and Start No Earlier Than (SNET) are the most popular ways of establishing deadlines and time constraints with CPM.

Estimating Duration

If you ever wondered why "estimates" is the word used for referring to setting the duration of different activities that comprise a project, wonder no more. This is because there's no foolproof way of determining the exact amount of time to complete each and every activity – you can only get a ballpark figure or an estimate of such, which is the scientific equivalent of guessing. It's akin to saying how long do you take a bath – there's no singular answer. Only estimates.

You can arrive at estimates using scientific methods so that you can be assured of relatively higher accuracy as compared to innocently guessing figures or plucking numbers from the sky. Estimating based on actual experience is a relatively simple yet scientific way of estimating durations. Applying a certain, acceptable probability makes it even better. As your acceptable probability increases, so will your estimation of duration be.

Upon getting an estimate, you consider your available resources for pushing through with activities and if the resources aren't up to par in terms of what's needed, then you increase the amount of time needed for successfully completing certain activities – their durations – to account for potential shortages in resources. Then, you factor in external factors that can impact your team's ability to successfully conduct activities by adding more time to your estimated duration. Lastly, it's better to pad the estimated duration further because chances are, any estimated duration submitted to superiors for approval always gets slashed regardless. By padding it at the onset, you increase the chances of your superiors approving your "real" estimated duration for activities and projects.

Duration

While duration often refers to the time needed to successfully complete an activity or project, it isn't limited to such a definition. It can also be expressed in terms of actual working time or the amount of time that's actually spent working on the activity or project, which excludes non-working time.

Man-hours is another way of expressing duration estimates, which is the amount of time – in hours – each person working on a certain activity needs to complete it. Lastly, duration can also be expressed in terms of "resource" time, which is the time needed by each unit or measure of resource that's needed for certain activities.

A point of contention when it comes to estimating activities or projects' estimated durations is whether to use actual experience or theoretical duration. If it sounds a bit technical, let me give you a personal example for illustration.

My friend can finish writing a 9,000-word book in one day, which means she can finish writing 5 such books from Monday to Friday, right? Not necessarily. Per her experience, the most number of such books she has actually finished in a workweek is 4. Why is her actual experience different from her theoretical duration for 5 books of 9,000 words each?

For one, life doesn't happen "theoretically" and many times, there are many curve balls thrown at us. In the case of my friend, errands for her mom and other social obligations as well as mental fatigue keep her from finishing anything more than 4 books in a work week. In this case, the "theoretical" isn't a good gauge for estimated duration. But if the activity is highly dependent on automated processes and resources, then theoretical can be a good estimate given that automated processes and resources aren't affected by subjective factors like mood, fatigue and social events.

Self-Fulfilling?

While many projects and activities are finished right on schedule or later, it's seldom we come across projects and activities that are completed earlier than the deadlines. Why is that so? Two things: procrastination and Parkinson's Law. I don't think I need to explain the procrastination part but I do believe I need to explain what Parkinson's Law is.

Parkinson's Law says that whatever amount of time you give to complete an assignment, you'll tend to maximize it. For some people, they want to submit the best possible assignment they can give so even if they finish ahead of time, they'll take the remaining time to review and further improve on their already finished works. Some people, well, they just procrastinate.

Chapter 8: Project Risk Management

Risk management can benefit your projects in many different ways. Dealing proactively with uncertain project events can help your project become highly profitable, which can result in minimizing the impact of specific threats to your projects. As such, you can seize most opportunities that come your projects' way.

It can also help you conclude your projects on time, within or even under budget without sacrificing quality results. Your team members will also be much happier if they don't have to constantly put out "fires" as a result of failures that could've been prevented in the first place.

In this chapter, we'll take a look at 10 ways of successfully applying risk management to your projects.

Make It an Integral Part of Projects

All the effective risk management practices and principles in the world of project management won't mean squat if you don't actually include them in your projects. You cannot reap the fruits of something you didn't even plant and for your projects, you'll need to incorporate risk management in your projects if you want to actually taste its benefits.

Many project managers scoff at the need for incorporating risk management in their projects and in the end, it's them who gets scoffed at when things happen – things that could've been prevented or whose effects could've been mitigated by basic risk management practices – because of failure to manage their projects' risks. Such managers are either ignorant or stubborn – neither of which describe you, right? Right!

While experience is a good teacher, it isn't a perfect one. In fact, it can even be a very expensive one and as such, let experience be your teacher of last resort. If you can learn without having to pay the steep tuition fees associated with learning through "experience", I highly recommend that you do so. It's for this reason that top companies hire people to do nothing all day, all month and all year round but to identify, monitor and mitigate risks.

Identify at The Onset

The first step towards incorporating risk management in all the projects you'll manage is to identify the risks involved. An open mind is required for you to be able to effectively do this because you'll need to be open to all possibilities of certain risks actually coming to past in the future. Many close-minded people failed to anticipate even the mere possibility of what happened in 2008 with the United States' subprime mortgage crisis. Most of the so-called experts never saw it coming simply because their minds were closed because of the prosperity at the time.

You can identify risks through 2 sources: people and paper. Let's talk about people first.

Basically, people include your team members with their personal expertise and experiences and experts who aren't part of your team but you can trust as reliable and competent due to their extensive experience and proven track records in the kinds of projects you're handling. Through interviews and brainstorming, you can glean insights as to potential booby traps or opportunities that may otherwise go unnoticed if you didn't consult other people.

Paper refers to documents of projects – past and current – that in more ways than one, identify certain project risks. While such risks may not always be explicitly mentioned, you can discover them by carefully reading between the lines.

Good places to start are previous projects' plans, cases and documented planning of resources, among others. Other good documentary sources to consider include your organization's Intranet, other project plans and other trusted specialty websites.

This begs the question: can you say you're able to all risks that can affect your projects before they materialize or happen? I don't think so. But if you diligently and wisely make use of different risk identification techniques and approaches, you have higher chances of discovering most of your projects' risks. And if you're able to manage well those you've identified, you free yourself and your team to tackle the unexpected risks that do materialize.

Choose Your (Risks) Battles

All the risks you've identified that can impact your projects can only do so if they actually happen or materialize. There will be times, however, that identifying, anticipating and mitigating the potential effects of such risks – should they materialize – may take more effort and time than simply dealing with situations as they happen. As such, part of an effective project risk management strategy is choosing your battles, i.e., the risks you'll want to proactively (pre-emptive) address and which ones you'll simply accept as they materialize. You can do this by estimating the probability of a particular risk coming to pass and it's possible impact on your projects. If both the effect and probability are high, it'll be wise to develop mitigating strategies for such risks and manage it. If both probability and impact are low, you may ignore it and choose not to fight (manage) it and instead, focus on those that really matter.

If you estimate the risk's probability is low and the potential effect is great or if the probability is high with low potential effect, carefully consider the risk using approaches that are more "formal", which can help you estimate the total effects of both the probability and potential impact, also known as the expected value of risk or EVR. You can estimate EVR by multiplying the potential effect (usually in monetary terms) of a particular risk by the probability of it happening.

Suppose for example that Risk A can result in additional project costs amounting to $5,000 with an 80% possibility of materializing. Your estimated EVR would then be $5,000 X 80%, which equals $4,000. What does this imply?   This means if you are going to take measures to mitigate Risk A, it shouldn't cost you more than $4,000, which is your EVR.

Communicate The Risks

Managers were frequently unaware of impending disasters in many situations where their projects failed. What's even more disturbing is the fact that someone from his or her team – from others in the organization even – was actually aware of such impending disasters but failed to inform the project manager concerned. In such cases, you can see the importance of being able to communicate risks clearly and effectively to project managers. So if you want your projects to succeed, you should ensure that your projects have clear and effective lines for communicating risks.

One way to do this is to simply include the act of communicating risks in all your projects' activities. For example, always bring up the subject of your projects' risks during team meetings. Don't make it the final item on the list – prioritize it! By prioritizing the discussion of risks in your team's meetings, you can cultivate a culture where risks are taken seriously in order to minimize the chances of them blowing up in the team's face and cause its projects to fail. And when discussing risks during your meetings, don't just focus on the existing ones you've already identified but also brainstorm for potential new ones.

Another way that you can establish good risk communication lines is to create a clear and direct line between you – as the project manager – and your superiors, project sponsors or principals. Focus all your risk communication efforts on the biggest and most significant risks and ensure that the parties mentioned are always updated on them so as not to surprise them. And when it comes to the biggest and most significant risks, its best to give the decision-making burdens to your superiors or project sponsors because often times, risks of such magnitude are often beyond your mandate as project manager.

Opportunities Too

Project risks are usually labeled as the bad guys, being the ones that can potentially harm projects. Today's modern approaches to risk management however also look at "positive" risks, i.e., opportunities. These are certain unexpected events that can prove to be beneficial for the projects you handle, even for the organization as a whole. These "positive" risks, also known as the good guys, can help you finish your projects better, faster, and even with bigger profits.

It's sad however, that many project teams barely make it to the finish line because normally, they're overloaded with tasks that need to be quickly finished. These situations are those where the focus is mostly, if not only, on risks (negatives, the bad guys). To balance things out and improve your chances of successfully finishing projects, make sure that you allot some time – even if it's for just half an hour – to also deal with and manage project opportunities. Chances are, you'll be able to discover hidden gems of opportunities that don't require much by way of time or resource investments but can give your projects big payoffs.

Risk Ownership

Most project managers believe that creating a list of risks that their projects face is all there is to it when it comes to risk management. They couldn't be any more wrong. Identifying and listing those risks is just the beginning. The next important step is to clearly identify the people who are accountable for managing such risks. Someone needs to bear the burden or responsibility of managing certain risks and be accountable for poor management of such, if ever.

Doing this can be very simple. Just assign every team member with the risks that you and your team have identified and listed. Then, that risk owner should be responsible for optimally managing such risk. While your team members may feel very uncomfortable at first, the beneficial effects for your projects will be worth it. And over time, they'll become used to it and learn to be good risk managers themselves.

Part of being accountable for certain risks include footing the bill for managing such risks poorly. And you'll need to communicate these clearly at the onset to minimize any chances of miscommunications and ultimately, mismanagement of assigned risks. The beautiful thing, if you may call it that, about making each and every risk owner foot the bill for the mismanagement of risks is that it makes them take risk management seriously.

When they know that they're going to pay for any negative results or losses arising from negligence in managing their assigned risks, they will do anything and everything to make sure that the risks assigned to them are managed well. While their motivations may be selfish, i.e., self-preservation, it ultimately redounds to the project's benefit. And this can be particularly useful when huge sums of money are on the line.

Prioritize

Many project managers make the mistake of treating risks the same as people: equally. While doing so can make life as a project manager really simple and easy, it may fail to optimize your projects' expected results.

This is because risks are more like smartphones - they're not created equal with some being more significant than others. Some risks you can just ignore because their probabilities and their potential negative impacts are negligible, which makes resource and time allocation for managing them rather impractical. On the other hand, some risks have very large potential negative impacts on your projects and even have high chances of materializing. As such, some risks would warrant careful risk management.

As with other important things in life, you'll need to choose your risk management battles well as a project manager so you can focus your team's resources, time and effort on those things that truly matter. Choose your battles wisely and you can significantly increase your chances of successfully completing your projects.

Analysis

As a project manager, your ability to understand the nature of your projects' risks is important for you to respond to them well. As such, you'll be better off taking some time to closely look at each of the risks that you and your team have identified and listed, and avoid jumping to conclusions about them without first analyzing them.

You can analyze your projects' risks at different levels. On an individual level, it's best to evaluate how they can affect your projects as well as what can make such risks happen. And after you've studied their potential effects, you can have an idea what can actually happen as soon as a particular risk materializes, including its other side effects. Analyzing your projects' risks in more detail can help you see the magnitude of each particular risk's effect on certain categories or activities of your projects such as quality, lead-time and costs.

Another way or level of analyzing your projects' risks is by looking at potential triggers or events that may take place prior to the manifestation of such risks. For this, you can list down the many different things and events that may increase or decrease the chances of such risks actually happening.

Another way to analyze your projects' risks is by looking at them from the perspective of the whole project. As a project manager, you will need to answer common questions about your projects such as how much is the required budget and when will your projects be finished. You can simulate the answers to these questions by taking the risks you identified into account. For example, you can simulate for how long the completion of your project will be delayed if a particular identified risk actually happens. You can do the same in terms of how your total project costs can be affected by certain risks.

You can gain valuable insights through the information that you gather as a result of analyzing your project risks. This process can also help you determine the necessary resources or activities that can help you optimally manage your project risks.

Responding to Risks

Well thought of and implemented risk responses can add value to your projects. Such can help you minimize the probability if your identified risks becoming real or reduce its potentially harmful effects on your projects. What's important here is how you execute your planned responses. The aforementioned steps or ways allow you to map, understand and prioritize your projects' risks but this one will help you respond well to them.

You basically have three options for responding to or dealing with your project identified risks: risk acceptance, risk minimization and risk avoidance. If a particular risk has minimal negative effects on your project or if it maybe very challenging, expensive and time consuming to manage, risk acceptance maybe the most logical approach.

Risk avoidance, on the other hand, means that you will change or reorganize your projects in ways that will allow you or your projects to stay clear of certain types of risk. Examples of these include using a certain type of technology, changing suppliers or simply terminating a project. There will be times that prudence may be the better part of valor and that humbling yourself by terminating a really bad project can be much better then losing much money on them just to save face.

Possibly the most popular or applicable of the responses or options is risk minimization. This is because in most cases, you don't have the option of accepting or avoiding certain types of risks if you are to successfully achieve your project objectives. And for risk minimization, the ability to analyze your risk somewhere can be very helpful. Getting insurance for key resources or installing good quality fire sprinklers to help control accidental fires quickly and efficiently are some good examples of minimizing risks.

Log Them

While this one's mostly about bookkeeping, it's worth taking into consideration as a project manager. What I mean by logging risks is to create and maintain a risk management logbook (or an electronic equivalent if you're more into high tech) that will help you to stay on top of your projects' risks by allowing you to easily view their progress and minimize your, pardon the pun, risks of forgetting or neglecting them.

You can also use your risk management log as a good way to communicate your projects' risk's actual status to your team members and stake holders.

What does a good risk management log look like? It's one that clearly describes each of the identified project risks, clearly identifies team members who own those risks (accountability) and helps you conducts basic analyses of potential causes and effects of such risks. While this may seem to be a very boring project management activity for you as a manager, believe me when I say that doing this risk-bookkeeping activity can give you and your projects great benefits in terms of risk management, most especially if you have identified quite a number of risks.

Don't give in to the temptation that many project managers face: ditching the risk management log. Many managers who do so do it for the wrong reasons such as making sure it's harder to put the blame for failed projects on them, among others. Such a belief is actually counterproductive because by not logging your projects' identified risks, the chances of your projects not being successfully completed are much higher and when your projects do fail, guess who's ultimately accountable for it? That's right – it's you as project manager!

Remember, maintaining a risk management log doesn't just help you ensure successfully completed projects. It also helps you look great as a project manager.

Monitor Risks and Related Tasks

Finally, monitoring risks and the tasks that they're associated with can help you minimize the chances of being hit by a curve ball because by doing this daily, you get to be on top of your identified risks' and tasks latest developments. You'll be able to successfully respond to your risks based on developments in either the risks themselves or the tasks associated with them.

Tracking risks focuses on identifying the risks that may have the highest chances of becoming real as well as their significance or magnitude. Doing this can help you – as project manager – be on top of your projects' most significant risks and add more value to your projects.

Chapter 9: Evaluating Your Projects' Results

Before we get into details about evaluating your projects' results, let's first define what evaluation really is. We can define evaluation as a systematic way of appraising the quality and success of your projects. When we say success, we talk about whether or not your projects' objectives are realized and when we talk about quality, we refer to whether or not your projects' stakeholders' needs have been met.

Basically, there are two ways to evaluate the results of your projects: formative and summative. Formative evaluation seeks to evaluate your projects' initial and ongoing activities with the intention of improving the work or activities that are already in progress. It also seeks to optimize the chances of your projects being completed successfully. Formative evaluation is done as your projects are being implemented at several points. Its components include:

- Needs Assessments: Identifying the parties who need the project, their particular needs and what activities can help fill those needs.

- Evaluability Assessments: Determining the feasibility of an evaluation and how your projects' stakeholders can affect its usefulness.

- Implementation Evaluations: Assessing if your projects are being implemented according to plans, with the idea that any effects can only be evaluated if your projects, including its components, are being implemented as planned.

- Progress Assessments: Assessing any progress made in terms of achieving your projects' objectives, which involves gathering of information to determine if key milestones we reached as well as to identify any developments that were unexpected.

On the other hand, summative evaluation is done to get an assessment of the impact and quality of your fully implemented projects and to verify whether or not the stated goals of your projects have been reached. As with formative evaluation, summative evaluation has a couple of components too, which include:

- Evaluation of outcomes: investigation of whether or not your projects had demonstrable effects on outcomes that we're particularly defined.

- Evaluation of impact: assessment of your projects' overall or total effects, regardless if intended or not, which includes effects over the long term.

- Cost evaluation: analyzing your projects' cost-benefit and cost-effectiveness aspects in order to evaluate financial efficiency through comparison of costs and outcomes related to your projects.

In the next 5 chapters (10 to 14), we'll will discuss in more detail the different areas of the project results evaluation process.

Chapter 10: Evaluation Of Results – Identifying Key Points

There are two ways that you can identify such points: through your projects' stakeholders' views on the necessary type of evaluation that needs to be done and your projects' underlying conceptual models.

Your points for evaluating your projects must contain the views of your projects' stakeholders, focusing on what they think is important to know during the evaluation. You can directly assess these points by simply asking them what are the key questions that they believe need to be answered during your projects' evaluations, being part of its evaluability assessments.

You can use logical models that can clearly show the entire processes beginning with your projects' inputs to their expected long-term results in order to capture your projects' conceptual models. These conceptual models can help foster a common understanding within the team of your projects' expected outcomes, connections and structures, which can greatly help in terms of focusing your project evaluations on the most important aspects only. It may be useful if you work backwards when developing your projects' conceptual models, i.e., beginning with your projects' desired outcomes and identifying the important events or situations needed to achieve such outcomes.

Questions, Indicators and Targets

Next, you'll need to come up with your projects' targets, indicators and questions for evaluations. The evaluation points you've generated from the first step will be your basis for coming up with relevant evaluation questions for process evaluation (the quality of your projects' implementations) and effects evaluation (your projects' successes).

The questions you'll ask for evaluating processes must be related to your projects' organization and planning of activities. These must focus on whether or not your projects' planned activities have been implemented per project plans, how challenges can be discovered during project implementations as well as how to best manage such challenges, and how your team can assure its projects' quality.

The questions you'll ask for evaluating your projects' effects must be related to its objectives, e.g., whether or not these were achieved, among others.

You'll also need to quantify your evaluation questions via indicators. Indicators that help you verify the timeliness as well as accuracy of your projects' planned activities or steps are called process indicators. Those that are related to levels of efficiency, user satisfaction and the project, among others, are called performance indicators. Indicators that are linked to the ability to achieve your projects' objectives are called effect indicators. It will be especially helpful for specifying multiple variables for each of your projects' objectives and measure their achievement levels if your projects' objectives are SMART – specific, measurable, achievable, realistic and time-bound.

The indicators you'll use for evaluating your projects' results must variables that are easily measurable, valid, repeatable, objective and reliable. As much as possible, such variables' values must be specific in terms of target quality level and expected numbers, among others, so that it can act as a benchmark for comparing your projects' results.

Design Selection

After you have finished formulating your projects' evaluation questions and defining their target values and indicators, you can proceed to choosing a particular design for your evaluation. In choosing such a design, you must consider the following:

- Cross-sectional or Longitudinal Design: Longitudinal studies collect data from the same subjects or sources but at different periods of time, e.g., prior to and after a particular course of action. Longitudinal designs are normally choses for methodological purposes but more often than not, these can be challenging in terms of linking the responses of individuals over time or looking for respondents that become unreachable or lost.

In cross-sectional studies, on the other hand, new subjects or samples are drawn every time data is collected. Because of the challenges inherent with longitudinal studies, cross-sectional designs for evaluation can be a good and viable alternative.

Another design choice related to the two is whether or not to use comparison groups for evaluating if outcomes are results of the activity or project.

- Samples: Larger sample sizes will make your evaluations more accurate due to reduced sampling errors, it can also affect your evaluations' validity with higher sample and response biases, which refer to biases resulting from loss of units for sampling and choosing samples that may not truly reflect the real results, respectively. As such, you as project manager will be better off prioritizing procedures that minimize these biases. This may mean going for methods that use a smaller number of samples.

– Data Collection Methods: You must choose between qualitative or quantitative methods – or combine both – for your project evaluations. Quantitative methods involve using surveys and questionnaires, actual records and data, counting or web logs. Qualitative methods for collecting data include focus groups, interviews, expert opinions or observations. Each method's adequacy isn't determined by the methods themselves but on their ability to match your projects' implementation contexts, answer the questions for evaluation and be in line with your projects' stakeholders' and target groups' expectations.

Chapter 11: Evaluation Of Results – Data Collection

After you've chosen an evaluation design, you must now proceed to collecting the necessary information in ways that address both political and technical issues. Let's consider political first.

What we refer to when we say political issues is the way you'll be collecting data within the context of your organization's policies and procedures and the sensitivities and needs of the participants from whom you may need to gather data from. It goes without saying that for you to be able to successfully gather existing recorded data from the different units in your organization, you'll need to first obtain the necessary permissions and clearances.

And if you're planning to involve participants in your data gathering endeavors, you'll need to clearly inform them about:

- How you will use the results;

- How the information that will be obtained from them will be kept in strict confidentiality and anonymity;

- How there'll be no repercussions whatsoever from any information that they may disclose during the evaluation; and

- How their prior consent will be an absolute must if there is really a need for disclosing sensitive information, however anonymous it may be.

If you're planning to involve more people in the data gathering activities, you must first train them to conduct the data gathering activities in an unbiased and objective manner. Categories or ratings of the data collected by each assessor for same projects or events must be compared. Their reliability must also be established. These may require your supervision so that objectivity will be ensured.

You can reduce biases in your samples by upping the number of your respondents, keeping in mind the trade-offs between reducing sampling error and biases, as mentioned earlier.

Lastly, your data collection activities must be as less intrusive and disruptive as possible. You should take into consideration the sensitivities and schedules of your target group respondents, changing your approach midway if situations call for it.

Chapter 12: Evaluation Of Results - Analysis

Now that you have the necessary data, it's time to analyze! How you'll analyze your data will be dependent on whether your data is quantitative or qualitative. Regardless of your choice of methods by which you'll analyze your data, you will need to perform these steps:

- First, you'll need to check your raw data for any potentially defective ones, such as those that are too far out or unlikely. This is to help ensure that defective or problematic data items are purged from your data set and ensure the quality of your evaluation.

- Next, you'll need to prime up or prepare the data you've collected for your analysis. You must enter and code them into your data set. Part of this process is ensuring the quality of your data set.

– Next, perform your initial analysis of the data per your evaluation plan. You can use different statistical analyses programs for quantitative data. For qualitative ones, more and more computer programs are becoming available for analyzing narrative types of data. Most of statistical analyses and evaluations are based on relatively simple tools for descriptive statistics such as mean, median, mode, frequencies and tests for statistical differences, among others. But for analyses that are more complex and are derived through cause-and-effect studies, you may have to use statistical tools that are equally as complex such as modeling using structural equations, regression analysis and variances. The good news is that all you really need to do is understand the basic concepts of such tools because you can just plug the data sets into computer programs, which will be doing the hard, complex and laborious work of analyzing and computing the data. Your work as project manager is to simply understand what the statistical results imply.

– Lastly, you'll need synthesize and integrate your statistical findings into a bigger context or a general framework. Using the results of statistical analysis and evaluation, you can draw conclusions about your projects' results and answer your questions for evaluation that you've created earlier. When apparent contradictions in results appear, they must be explained or studied further.

Chapter 13: Reporting Of Results

The last step, right after you've analyzed and evaluated your projects' results, is reporting your findings to your concerned stakeholders. Doing this will require you to gather all collected data that was used in the evaluation, refining your findings in order to answer your evaluation questions clearly and accurately, and distributing the results of your evaluation to the concerned stakeholders.

Your evaluation report must contain, among its numerous sections, the background of the evaluation conducted, your evaluation questions, the selected evaluation methods and designs, statistical methods used for analysis, the results or findings of the analysis and your conclusions based on such findings or results. You must present the necessary information in styles and manners that aren't merely appropriate but also compelling and appealing to your reports' target audiences. And speaking of different audiences, you may need to present your report in ways that can best be appreciated and understood by different audience groups. For example, your organization's Board of

Directors may require only the general conclusions and explanations for such while the departments or units concerned in terms of making the necessary changes you've outlined in your evaluation report will need a more detailed and technical version.

Chapter 14: Practical Issues Concerning Evaluation Of Results

Staff skills

Planning an evaluation, selecting an evaluation design, collecting data, analyzing and interpreting them requires specific knowledge and skills. When these are not available in the project organization, evaluation can be outsourced to an external evaluator. Outsourcing has pros and cons: while it is likely to enhance the quality and objectivity of the evaluation, add to the project status, and take away the practical burden of carrying out the evaluation, it also reduces the ownership of the evaluation results, may give rise to conflicts over priorities, and reduces the opportunity to learn from the project. Whether or not the evaluation should be done by experts depends on its scope. Small-scale evaluations focusing on formative aspects of a project can mostly be undertaken by organizations themselves. Large-scale, complex evaluation designs, on the other hand, require more expertise to design the study, select the instruments and manage the data collection and analysis.

Budget

Project evaluation can be costly, particularly if it aims to capture various aspects of both the process and outcomes of the project. Evaluation should therefore be incorporated in the project's budget in a way that makes the evaluation study realistic, manageable, efficient, and productive.

Timing

It is a common mistake to assume that evaluation takes place at the end of a project. Although the effects of a project are usually achieved at the end, evaluation must be planned from the outset and conducted throughout the project lifetime. The scope, complexity and quality of the evaluation design will affect the time needed for data collection and analysis. It is important to plan enough time for the evaluation, taking into consideration the requirements of the methods envisaged. A survey requires considerable time to create and pretest questions and to obtain high response rates. Qualitative methods may be time consuming because data collection and analysis overlap, and the analysis gives rise to new evaluation questions. If insufficient time is allowed for evaluation, it may be necessary to curtail the amount of data to be collected or to cut short the analytic process, thereby limiting the value of the findings. For evaluations that operate under severe time constraints—for example, where budgetary decisions depend on the findings—choosing the best method can present a serious dilemma.

Chapter 15: How a Good Manager Closes a Project

How do you wind up your project and leave a good mark on everyone involved? Certainly, not by ordering the closing of the facility one fine morning and flying away to issue a press statement! You have been working with a team of dedicated people, consulting with enthusiastic, or even fearful, stakeholders, and you need to think of them as you prepare to wind up operations.

For sure you wouldn't wish to leave a bitter taste in their mouths when you are still in business, because you never know if you'll need them in the future for endorsement on other projects. And even at a personal level, when you work closely with people you get to build a relationship that you don't want to mess up unnecessarily.

So, how does a good manager conduct the closing stage of the project?

Makes it major

Well, how major your closing is going to be will be relative, of course, depending on the size of your project, its nature and so on. A government sponsored public facility, for instance, may be expected to have a closing more formal than a private project; while that of a public project of the nature of the Olympics is bound to be more pompous than most other projects. In short, we are adopting the same working principle we mentioned earlier on in the book, of being flexible; avoiding rigidity in order to embrace suitability.

The main message to take away from here is that your project needs a definitive closing point. Let it be seen that the consumer, or whoever is representing the consumer, has accepted the project as it is; that any changes or modifications that were meant to be effected have been effectively made to everyone's satisfaction; and that no complaints will be expected later on.

Defines the closing point

If you are in charge of the Olympics, for example, you need to make everyone understand the point at which you are going to wind up everything – a point when you shouldn't expect sports action in the field or communication between

Olympics officials and the sports teams; a point at which everyone in the field can engage in private discussions without affecting the efficient running of the Olympics.

You surely don't want to be that project manager who only tells the team on the ground that the project is over when the foreman calls to ask for the team's wages for the day. So you'd be paying for a day of idling, during which the foreman gave the team members odd tasks to keep them busy. In short, a project should not be left to drift without a foreseen end. At the same time, the closing of a project should not be shocking to employees and other stakeholders – people showing up at work in full uniform only for you to tell them, oh no, it's over though I never mentioned it earlier... All stakeholders need to have a clear closing point to look forward to.

Makes it a fruitful process

We have already alluded to the fact that it is not good to leave the project arena like a thief nor should you close shop abruptly – unless, of course, there is an emergency of catastrophic nature. What you need to do is have a discussion with all stakeholders, where each party gets an opportunity to express their feelings and also reservations if they have any; make a thorough evaluation of the completed project against planned standards; and finally wait to see the project approved and accepted.

Plans the activities that mark the closing stage

As a good manager, it is expected that you are aware of the activities that need to be done during the closing stage. The words *closing* and *shutting* may have a common meaning in grammar, but when it comes to the context of closing a project, you cannot equate it to shutting premises' doors and leaving. You have reports to make, for example, to the organization executive board, program management, or such other oversight bodies. Then, you have, of course, to await their authorization, and if they need a presentation, you've got to have some people ready to provide it.

Then there is the actual deed of authorizing the closure of the project. And, depending on the kind of project it is, you may need to organize an authorization ceremony. A good project manager plans for all that and does not wait to fumble at the last minute to organize the relevant closing activities.

Is ready for the most important closing activities

This readiness entails being prepared to handle the five most important aspects of project closing. These activities include:

- Planned winding up of the project

- Winding up of a premature nature

- Handing over of the output

- Evaluating the project

- Final move of recommending the project closure

Is competent enough to tell when the project has fulfilled its purpose

A good project manager need not wait till the project sponsor or any of the other stakeholders finds fault with project specifications and other issues. The project manager needs to see to it that work has been done according to plan and that any deviations have been explained and accepted before project closing time.

Plans for the relevant mode of product handover

A good project manager understands when he or she is handling a project that requires product handover to take place in phases and when it only requires one massive handover right at the end of project life. The manager is also competent to prepare for the handover without interfering with the project budget and other normal operations.

Is competent to handle premature closing of a project

Much as you may dread premature closing of a project, the

reality is that it sometimes happens of necessity. If a big earthquake was predicted, for example, and it was thought that the location of your geothermal project was going to be affected, would you surely continue pouring more and more resources to the project or you'd prepare for emergency project closing? A good project manager should be able to weigh situations and come up with the most cost-effective way of closing the project at that premature stage.

Secures relevant signatures

Surely if you were using hired equipment for your project, would it not be prudent for you to ensure the property is returned to its rightful owners as you prepare to close the project; and that the rental company signs the relevant papers to indicate that you owe them nothing? A good project manager understands the documents that require qualified lawyers to sign and those require suppliers and other stakeholders to sign – and those signatures are secured well before the last act of project closure.

Shows appreciation to everyone concerned

A good project manager understands that credit for a successful project goes to everyone in the team. As such it is a great idea to mark the closing of the project by organizing some celebration for the team and the main stakeholders. It leaves everyone feeling good that their contribution was noted and admired. Who doesn't like some motivation, anyway?

Chapter 16: How to Identify a Great Project Manager

Let's just say, great project managers cannot be identified by their manner of dressing or manner of speaking. Granted those may give you an idea of the individual's personality, but it takes more than what is visible to make a great project manager. We may, indeed, have to make do with just good managers.

Here are some tips that will help you improve as a project manager

Exuding authority

The aura of authority of a great project manager exudes naturally. And that makes the team listen and take their message seriously. Great project managers also happen to be optimistic; and when someone discusses the way forward authoritatively, it helps the project advance faster. One of the reasons a great project manager commands authority is that the organization's management, colleagues, as well as those below him or her views the project manager in good light. In short, even if you were naturally a confident person, but then the people you work with did not think much of you, your self-confidence would wane.

When management likes you and you ask for their support, for example, it's bound to come relatively easily. And when a good project manager directs their team in a certain way, they trust that it's for the good of everyone concerned; and the project, of course. In short, for a project manager, it is good to have someone whom the organization values for their charisma, optimism and enthusiasm; and one who has the respect of everyone else involved.

Ability to sort out things

A good project manager is capable of sifting through whatever material is available in a flash, and identifying that which warrants a second look and that which needs to be discarded or totally ignored. If you enlist the services of a project manager who looks at mounds of data as a great resource, you are in trouble. For a project to succeed, what you need is not lots of data but availability of important data. So a good project manager should be able to tell what is extraneous and what is really useful and worth retaining. In any case, trying to deal with too much information can be overwhelming.

Competent in prioritizing

If you are set on attending every invitation that lands on your table, be it invitations to meetings, official parties or any other form of function, your work will be adversely affected. For one, as a project manager, you need to be visible to your team members and available to give your take on various issues affecting the project, and if you attend unnecessary functions, then you'll not be easily accessible to your team.

And even when it comes to e-mails, a good project manager is able to single out those that he or she should personally handle and those that can be handled by an assistant or someone else. After all, these avenues end up bombarding you with more and more information and you need to limit your data input to protect yourself from possible overwhelm.

Being a great listener

A good project manager does not just appear to listen but actually does pay attention to other people, and take note of other people's sentiments. Those are the ones that the project manager considers on going back to the project site. In fact, because of the project manager's ability to grasp what other people feel about things, he or she is able to pose helpful questions to those people. This kind of communication brings out pertinent issues that may have the potential to affect the project either positively or negatively. And that is really great feedback for the project manager.

Not using information as a form of weapon

How much do you suffer from self confidence that you should withhold information from others for fear that it may empower them? Surely your strength as a project manager should not emanate from other people appearing weak. Rather, you need to be able to be distinguishable even when being among competent people.

Good project managers disseminate information as they receive it as long as it is relevant to the project. That way, individual team members can use the information creatively and help advance the cause of the project. A mark of a great project manager is the ability and willingness to volunteer information and pass it on to the stakeholders in a clear and concise manner.

Adhering to communication schedules

Why do you agree to a schedule of meetings, project briefings and so on, if you are not ready to avail yourself? A good project manager keeps to planned meetings and project appraisal sessions as planned. It is demoralizing for team members who attend scheduled sessions only to find that some key people are not in attendance. Not only are the agendas adversely affected when the project manager fails to attend, but it is a blow to the morale of the rest of the team.

Has reasonable relevant expertise

Of course for a project manager to pass as being good, it is important to possess general managerial skills. However, besides those generic skills of a project manager, it helps when he or she has some in-depth knowledge of some important expertise being employed in the project. Don't you, for instance, think that a person with medical background would be better placed to lead a project related to containment of an epidemic?

Being a consensus builder

Much as you want skilled and competent people on your project team, sometimes they can also have strong personalities that tend to pose extreme competition amongst themselves. This is where a good project manager comes in and exercises great consensus building skills. You need people to be on the same page every step on the way as they work on the project, and so conflicts are a distraction nobody can afford. A good project manager ensures that conflicts are resolved in a way that does not injure people's egos and one which, for most part, reflects a win-win resolution; all for the benefit of the project.

Having great networks; both formally and informally

At a formal level, it is fine to have a project manager who has great rapport with people in his or her league; people who have handled similar projects and succeeded. Consulting with such people give great insight to the project and helps the project manager to avoid possible hurdles before the team begins to stumble.

A great project manager also has the capacity to pick helpful information from people not directly engaged with the project. For example, when there is a peace keeping mission at some part of the world, the officer in charge of such a project does not rely only on official feedback; he also relies on feedback from local residents. And the combination of official and unofficial feedback enriches the project manager resource pool as far as usable information for decision making goes.

Enthusiasm in the work

Which team member will be enthusiastic working under a project manager who is taking the project as a burden rather than an undertaking that he or she looks forward to doing? Enthusiasm is somewhat contagious; so if your project manager is enthusiastic about the project, the feeling is spread amongst the rest of the team.

A good project manager takes the project as a worthy challenge, and is excited about working on it, looking forward to great results. In fact, great project managers make a career of project management, even taking additional training to polish their skills. The life of a great project manager is one of excitement emanating from the positive challenges faced on a consistent basis. Still, great project managers are a rare gem; the reason there is need to keep reading material on good project management and practicing the skills taught.

Chapter 17: What Challenges Do Project Managers Face?

What would make a project manager encounter challenges, yet an organization (presumably) identifies a qualified person for the role? Well, there are a number of reasons, not least the fact that a project manager has to deal with the most complex of elements in the center of any project – namely, the element of time; that of money; of scope; and also of people. The project manager has to balance the importance and role of each of these elements. No wonder many project managers keep going for refresher courses to upgrade their skills, particularly those skills that help to deal with unexpected project hitches.

That introduction, as you can see, presumes that the project is being led by a competent project manager. Unfortunately, this is not always the case. And that is one reason this book is important – to show you what to look for in a project manager, in order to be able to tell if the person is competent for the role or not.

A senior member of Consulting Services & Project Management Office, Sudhir Verma, has been quoted as expressing concern in the way people often prepare for project management. She says that organizations often put more emphasis on identifying the right resources and relegate the importance of identifying a suitable project manager to the periphery. In short, great resources and hospitable stakeholders minus a competent project manager cannot pull off a great project.

In any case, a skilful project manager saves you from another big mistake of thinking that some people involved in the project are of no consequence. A good project manager knows that nothing is far from the truth and that even the least paid person can make a move to sabotage your multi-million dollar project. As such, a competent project manager takes the initiative to bring everyone involved in the project on board so that they take pride in the project and do their best, not just to develop it, but also to protect it.

In fact, these stakeholders, who include the project team members, are the best placed individuals to promote your cause. And, of course, a project manager who understands the sensitivity of a project knows better than to alienate top personnel at management level. If they delay approval for funds and other requests, you are done, no matter how good you are. That is why it is important to shop well for a project manager so that your project runs smoothly.

Here is a list of challenges project managers face within a corporate set-up:

Having unclear goals

It is very difficult to work with unclear goals. For one, if you are given the role of leading a project and you are not told exactly what the expected end result is, good as you may be as a project manager, you can't make it happen – at least not in the way it should. It is important that you ask the right questions to be able to derive the necessary information, because if you don't do that, it will be your problem moving forward to spell out the goals to other stakeholders. How can you even get people to support your project if you can't spell out its goals to them?

Changing goal posts

This is not a football pitch we are talking about, but changing of original project scope. Just because you have good rapport with all stakeholders, including the clients, is no reason to factor in every suggestion that they make to you after the project has begun. Of course, there are those changes you can admit depending on the project management methodology you are using, but you need to be able to evaluate each request on its own merit and be firm if it is not possible to implement it.

Otherwise modifying the scope of your project haphazardly can be detrimental to the success of your project – raising costs beyond the budget; alienating people on the ground; and causing unnecessary delays on project completion. In short, scope creep is only to be allowed when it is absolutely necessary and when it is feasible to do so. To ensure that everyone is at peace with the project changes you are effecting, it is advisable that you communicate clearly and effectively to them, and in good time – actually before the changes begin.

Lack of relevant skills

It is difficult to take a project successfully through its successive phases when the people working on different processes are not competent enough to produce high standard results. In effect, the project manager may have to recommend training for those workers. And, of course, to be able to identify employees who are not up to par as well as those who are trainable, the project manager needs to possess great managerial skills.

In some cases, a project manager may need to outsource manpower if the organization does not have enough people who are skilled enough to work on the project. Other times, the project manager may just recommend hiring of additional people with relevant project skills.

Having team members who don't take responsibility

If the people you are working with do not own up when they have messed up, it becomes difficult for the project manager, not only to identify the point of project weakness, but also to direct advice where it is mostly needed.

Besides, when individuals avoid taking responsibility for their deeds, a blame game begins within the team and all hell breaks loose. If the project manager is to retain his or her respectable image, it is important to take control, bring the finger pointing to an end and get everyone working as a team. A good project manager needs to be able to get the team to adopt the spirit of brotherhood and sisterhood, where one person's weakness is everyone's weakness; in which case everyone does their best to make the weak links strong.

Poor planning against risk

Does it always rain at the exact place and time as the weather people tell everyone? Sometimes it truly does but often there are variations. Sometimes it floods when the forecast just mentioned rain in normal terms while other times the sun scotches the grass whereas the weather forecasting just pointed at a dry spell. Yet people do not panic and abandon their homes without a plan. What they do is call the relevant authorities who then dash to restore the area; send evacuation helicopters where necessary, and do what emergency situations call for in terms of humanitarian assistance. What are we learning here? The lesson is that counties and cities have emergency plans in place.

That is the same way a great project manager operates – having contingency plans in place so that should one action fail, you fall onto a substitute plan. However, in situations where senior management reckons that the project is expensive enough without adding the cost of risk management, the project manager has a hard time. Only a skilled project manager can help such a situation, making all stakeholders understand the importance of risk management and pushing through for a risk management plan. A good project manager is also able to identify the areas of the project that are most sensitive and require having solid risk management measures in place.

Failure to make contingency plans clear

Is it alright to set funds aside for use when things go wrong? Of course, it is; but it isn't enough. Often organizations spare money and call it a contingency fund without spelling out what measures would be taken if specific things happened. So when something happens, say if a boiler within the factory blows, it takes time to decide if it should be repaired or replaced. If residential areas for the project team become inhabitable, for some reason, nobody can tell if the team should be evacuated to a hotel and be accommodated there for the remaining part of the project or if some home should be leased for them.

Since it is not feasible to cater for every imaginable mess that could happen, a good project manager solicits input from team members in identifying the most risky areas of the project; and then plans specifically for them. In fact, when a contingency plan is specific, it is easy to modify it to suit another specific problem if the problem that arises is in a different area of the project.

Failure to communicate well

If things are not being communicated to you in good time, you have a problem as a project manager. However, it is the project manager's duty to ensure that there is efficient flow of information both horizontally and vertically. If top corporate management decides that your project cannot be funded if any changes are effected, someone needs to communicate that information to you. Yet sometimes it doesn't happen.

So the onus is on you to follow up and ask what the position is; and then you take it upon yourself to communicate that feedback to relevant stakeholders in good time. In any case, it is expected that a good project manager has the ability to communicate effectively both orally and in writing. There is something good about smooth flow of information, including making people feel valued. It is, definitely, a morale booster.

Setting unrealistic timelines

Can you strike a rock with a rod and derive water from it? Well, some prophet in the Holy Bible is said to have done that some centuries ago, but those were the days of miracles. In this realistic world, trying to demand that your team does the impossible will not just frustrate you but paralyze them to inertia. If you are in Johannesburg at 7am, for instance, and someone demands that you be at JFK Airport in two hours' time, what you do is simply shake your head and remain seated. You'll simply be a non-starter as far as taking the trip from South Africa to the US is concerned.

This analogy simply shows you the futility of exaggerating expectations or setting unrealistic deadlines. When this trend continues, team members get demoralized and productivity falls drastically. Ultimately, you cannot complete the project as per initial plan. Remember failure to perform well on a project reflects badly on the project manager.

Insufficient funding

If you needed $10 to buy ingredients to make a meal for a couple of friends, what phase of the preparation would you accomplish first if your provider gave you $3 first and promised to give you the rest in two more installments of $4 and $3 respectively? The point is some mode of funding is just ridiculously difficult to work with. In our case, you can't buy half a loaf in the morning and a few ounces of celery in preparation, as you wait to buy another half loaf later and possibly some tomatoes. You can't even formulate in your mind what kind of meal you'll be able to make at the end of the day!

It is for that reason that good project managers ask for upfront funding when it comes to preparing for a project. When you are deprived of resources at the right time, it becomes almost impossible to plan with confidence. You need to be sure of your funding to be able to prioritize the project functions.

Apathy on the part of stakeholders

Surely, how do you expect stakeholders to be enthusiastic if you don't tell them what is happening with the project? And that is a common weakness when working in big organizations. Management thinks it is enough that they are doing something good for everyone. It isn't; and people who stand to benefit from your project can end up being the same ones sabotaging it.

It is important that the project manager opens up communication channels amongst the project team and between the team and other stakeholders. That way, the stakeholders have an avenue through which they can express their reservations, give feedback and even state their preferences. The team also finds a way to explain why they are doing what they are doing and also what they plan to achieve and how it is going to benefit the people concerned.

Conclusion

Now that you understand what Project Management is, you need to practice applying the skills you have learnt in this book. You need to take every undertaking that you embark on as a project, and try to conduct yourself as efficiently as you can. In the process, you are likely to identify and classify appropriately the hitches that you encounter. When you do, try to apply the skills that you have learnt in this book on good project management, and see how well you are able to overcome those hitches. This is a great way of ensuring you practice good project management on a daily basis. In due course, you will be so confident that you can take up the role of project manager at a moment's notice without a worry.

The next step is for you to go through this book again, see if you took in all the tips provided, and think of real life situations where those tips are best applied. You are likely to realize that challenges that looked insurmountable earlier on can be easily tackled with a good system in place as shown in this book.

Made in the USA
Columbia, SC
10 January 2018